MESSAGE OF THE FATHERS OF THE CHURCH
General Editor: Thomas Halton

Volume 10

MESSAGE OF THE FATHERS OF THE CHURCH

THE GOSPEL & ITS PROCLAMATION

by

Robert D. Sider

 Michael Glazier, Inc.
Wilmington, Delaware

ABOUT THE AUTHOR

Robert D. Sider received his doctorate in patristic studies from Oxford University in 1965. He is Charles A. Dana Professor of Classical Languages at Dickinson College. Among his publications is *Ancient Rhetoric and the Art of Tertullian*. He is currently editing two volumes on the New Testament scholarship of Erasmus.

First published in 1983 by Michael Glazier, Inc.
1723 Delaware Avenue, Wilmington, Delaware 19806

Library of Congress Catalog Card Number: 83-81841
International Standard Book Number:
   Message of the Fathers of the Church series:
      (0-89453-312-6, Paper; 0-89453-340-1, Cloth)
THE GOSPEL AND ITS PROCLAMATION
      (0-89453-321-5, Paper)
      (0-89453-350-9, Cloth)

Cover design by Lillian Brulc

Printed in the United States of America

For
Catherine, Michael, and Robert

TABLE OF CONTENTS

EDITOR'S INTRODUCTION

The *Message of the Fathers of the Church* is a companion series to The *Old Testament Message* and The *New Testament Message.* It was conceived and planned in the belief that Scripture and Tradition worked hand in hand in the formation of the thought, life and worship of the primitive Church. Such a series, it was felt, would be a most effective way of opening up what has become virtually a closed book to present-day readers, and might serve to stimulate a revival in interest in Patristic studies in step with the recent, gratifying resurgence in Scriptural studies.

The term "Fathers" is usually reserved for Christian writers marked by orthodoxy of doctrine, holiness of life, ecclesiastical approval and antiquity. "Antiquity" is generally understood to include writers down to Gregory the Great (+604) or Isidore of Seville (+636) in the West, and John Damascene (+749) in the East. In the present series, however, greater elasticity has been encouraged, and quotations from writers not noted for orthodoxy will sometimes be included in order to illustrate the evolution of the Message on particular doctrinal matters. Likewise, writers later than the mid-eighth century will sometimes be used to illustrate the continuity of tradition on matters like sacramental theology or liturgical practice.

An earnest attempt was made to select collaborators on a broad inter-disciplinary and inter-confessional basis, the chief consideration being to match scholars who could handle the Fathers in their original languages with subjects in which they had already demonstrated a special interest and competence. About the only editorial directive given to the

9

selected contributors was that the Fathers, for the most part, should be allowed to speak for themselves and that they should speak in readable, reliable modern English. Volumes on individual themes were considered more suitable than volumes devoted to individual Fathers, each theme, hopefully, contributing an important segment to the total mosaic of the Early Church, one, holy, catholic and apostolic. Each volume has an introductory essay outlining the historical and theological development of the theme, with the body of the work mainly occupied with liberal citations from the Fathers in modern English translation and a minimum of linking commentary. Short lists of Suggested Further Readings are included; but dense, scholarly footnotes were actively discouraged on the pragmatic grounds that such scholarly shorthand has other outlets and tends to lose all but the most relentlessly esoteric reader in a semi-popular series.

At the outset of his *Against Heresies* Irenaeus of Lyons warns his readers "not to expect from me any display of rhetoric, which I have never learned, or any excellence of composition, which I have never practised, or any beauty or persuasiveness of style, to which I make no pretensions." Similarly, modest disclaimers can be found in many of the Greek and Latin Fathers and all too often, unfortunately, they have been taken at their word by an uninterested world. In fact, however, they were often highly educated products of the best rhetorical schools of their day in the Roman Empire, and what they have to say is often as much a lesson in literary and cultural, as well as in spiritual, edification.

St. Augustine, in *The City of God* (19.7), has interesting reflections on the need for a common language in an expanding world community; without a common language a man is more at home with his dog than with a foreigner as far as intercommunication goes, even in the Roman Empire, which imposes on the nations it conquers the yoke of both law and language with a resultant abundance of interpreters. It is hoped that in the present world of continuing language barriers the contributors to this series will prove opportune interpreters of the perennial Christian message.

PREFACE

The story of our Christian faith begins, in effect, with proclamation. Jesus came into Galilee with a message of good news—the "Kingdom of God" is at hand. The high drama of this proclamation, betrayed even in the spare narrative of Mark, is deftly exploited by both Matthew and Luke who expand upon and illustrate the message, Matthew in the Sermon on the Mount where the total inversion of all accepted values still catches the perceptive reader in surprise, shock and dismay; Luke with a tense narrative of the first moment of corporate decision to reject the divine Herald. The first records of the Apostolic age, too, set the proclamation of the message in center-stage of Christian history. And as in the Gospels, so in the *Book of Acts* and the Epistles, the message is set before us in a living context of drama—of surprise and tension, gratitude and hostility. Peter's first message at Pentecost emerges from a narrative whose very style reflects the effervescence of the miracle of tongues. The letters of Paul reveal the insecurities betrayed, the antagonisms aroused, by his effort to plant the message in the Gentile heart. Scholars may abstract the thematic "content" of the earliest Christian message—as has indeed been so graciously done in C.H. Dodd's seminal *The Apostolic Preaching and its Development* (Chicago, 1937)—but we cannot fully understand the message apart from the living context in which it was presented.

11

It seems therefore appropriate that in the present series on
The Message of the Fathers, one volume should be devoted
to a broad range of questions about the proclamation of the
Gospel: what were the modes in which it was presented?
How far did the audience shape its form and content? What
are the living contexts in which it sought its hearers? What
developments in content did it undergo? These are the central questions which have directed this study. In answering
these questions, our narrative has made no attempt to be
exhaustive, or profound. I have attempted rather to assemble material which is obvious—but primary—and through
it to give answers which are illustrative, sometimes
tentative.

The evidence which is available suggests that for early
Christianity, indeed even for the New Testament period, the
Gospel message was frequently conveyed not by Apostles
and prophets, but by artisans and merchants, men and
women of the work-a-day world, who presented the message to their neighbors by word and deed, by holy living and
holy dying, dying sometimes the death of martyrdom. First,
therefore, we investigate some of the evidence which reveals
the early Christians proclaiming the message in their daily
lives. Obviously, most of the material for our subject comes
in literary forms whose aims are sharply focused, and it is
with these that we must chiefly be concerned throughout
this book. From a literary point of view the early Church
was remarkably creative, so that not only is the bulk of the
material on which we might draw, vast, but its forms manifold. Guided as a principle of selection by the desire to focus
as closely as possible on the context in which, and especially
on the audience to which, the message was directed, I have
invited the reader, in the second place, to consider the
message as it was presented to non-Christians, to the Jew
first, and also to the Greek. The sequel then becomes inevitable: the reader will want to know how those still Jew, still
Greek, still non-Christian but eager to learn and eventually
ready to convert, were addressed; and finally, how the message was presented to those who through baptism had
become "the faithful." The limits of space have allowed us to

offer only a few fleeting glimpses of the presentation of the message to the faithful. For this, the selections have been chosen somewhat arbitrarily, on the basis of what appeared to be their potential interest. Still these glimpses are essential if we are to keep our subject in perspective: the good news is the message, and the good news belongs above all to the faithful.

Four notes of clarification may be helpful at this point. First, I have arranged the material primarily in terms of audience, defining the audience as Jewish, pagan, catechumens (learners) and the "faithful." We know that the early Christians were sensitive to the needs of individuals and groups within various audiences. These were the learned and the unlearned, the rich and the poor, Romans and non-Romans. Catechists were taught to adjust the message to the interests and status of each person. Among the faithful, more than one message was directed to the rich. But it was impractical within the limits of this book to categorize the material in relation to all the possible variations in audience. If today we place a strong emphasis in speaking the message to various classes and interest groups within our society, the evidence suggests this was less so in the early Church. The materials I have assembled demonstrate, I believe, that the early Church viewed the primary audiences to be Jews, pagans, catechumens, and full-fledged Christians. Second, it is important to state here what I shall recall in the text, that while early Christian literature usually had in each case a fairly well-defined primary audience, it was often assumed that its readers would extend well beyond those for whom it was chiefly intended. Thus literature designed to convert the Jew or the pagan often served to confirm the faith of Christians. Indeed some of the "apologetic literature" was directed in the first instance to Christians, though it was clearly expected that pagans would read it. The heart of the message, after all, remained the announcement of the Kingdom—the Rule of God—and at one level this remained the same for Christian and non-Christian. Third, I have wished to emphasize the continuity, as well as the development, of the proclamation from New

Testament times to the early fifth century. I have accordingly stressed wherever possible the New Testament antecedents. Finally, I have defined our period of investigation as the first four centuries of Christian life. In a topic so broad, severe limits must be imposed, but it seemed essential to carry the story as far as Augustine in the West and Chrysostom in the East.

It is one of the aims of the series that the Fathers should be allowed to speak for themselves. Hence the large proportion of extracts from the Fathers in this book. I have tried to limit my own narrative, providing only what seemed essential if the reader was to become aware in any significant sense of the living drama of the context in which the message was presented, and of the issues to which it was addressed. Dates can often be profitably generalized, and only where it seemed unavoidable have I raised questions of authenticity and attribution. Bibliographical notes suggest readings for each chapter, but those interested in pursuing in detail available scholarship on authors and texts should consult standard bibliographies on the subject.

I frankly confess that few tasks have afforded me greater pleasure than the translation of the passages which follow. I have tried to be faithful both to the language of the author and to the linguistic expectations of the modern reader. At times I have followed fairly closely the Latin and the Greek, finding English equivalents almost word for word. At the other extreme, I have not avoided an occasional paraphrase where it seemed the only reasonable way to express clearly the author's intent. I have done the translation at Dickinson College, and have been fortunate to have at hand in its library Migne's great *Patrologia.* I have not, however, relied on it exclusively, but have used modern critical editions whenever I could reasonably obtain them. Direct quotations from the Bible are taken from the Revised Standard Version.

I must express my great admiration for my secretary, Barbara McDonald, who was able to read my manuscript without error and who always met gracefully the impossible deadlines I set her in typing it.

I acknowledge with thanks a grant from the Research and Development fund of Dickinson College for expenses incurred in research, and in typing the manuscript.

Abbreviations:

CCL	Corpus Christianorum, Series Latina
CSEL	Corpus Scriptorum Ecclesiasticorum Latinorum
OECT	Oxford Early Christian Texts
PG	Patrologia Graeca
PL	Patrologia Latina
SC	Sources Chrétiennes
TU	Texte und Untersuchungen

References are generally by volume number and page or column.

Chapter One

THE DYNAMICS OF
PERSONAL ENCOUNTER

After the age of the Apostles, we hear relatively little of professional and itinerant missionaries, and we must conclude that the growth of Christianity proceeded through witnesses of other kinds. We have considerable evidence of the power in the silent witness of the life of individual Christians, and indeed of their death, at least by martyrdom. We also have accounts of the effect of the spoken witness by one individual to another, or to a small group; and of the effect simply of reading the Scriptures. A fair number of conversion stories have come down to us which offer us some insight into the dynamics of everyday personal encounters of pagans with the Christian message. Some of these are authentic personal confessions, others possibly fictional or idealizations of real events, and it is not always possible for us to distinguish. Nor is it essential for our purposes, if we understand that all such narratives describe the perceptions of how the message was, or ought to have been, presented to the unbeliever.

A Christian's Witness in the Family

The most intimate context for both the silent and the spoken witness was the family. The conversion singly of a husband or wife from heathen idolatry to Christian monotheism created an inevitable opportunity for witness in word and deed, for in antiquity domestic, social and political life was everywhere informed by idolatrous practices, while standards of pagan morality frequently violated the sanctity of mutual trust. Christian behavior stood out in sharp contrast to the customary ways of the pagans, and necessarily called attention to the faith which motivated it. Not that the witness thus afforded was always perceived as the shining light it was intended to be; indeed, it seems often to have been misunderstood, and perhaps with some reason. A Christian woman, for example, who refused to participate in traditional rituals associated with family feasts or community festivals, whose life challenged contemporary values and mores, and who identified with a strange community might be regarded not only by her husband but by servants also not as sweet, pure and devout, but as morose, difficult, even rebellious. In Apuleius' *Metamorphoses* we have the description from a pagan point of view of a woman who very possibly was a Christian.

> IX.14.[1] The baker who had bought me, though himself a fine and virtuous man, had a wife who was positively the worst woman ever. She subjected him to the most agonizing tortures of domestic life, and I often groaned silently for his fate. There was not a single vice that monstrous woman did not possess. Every abomination flowed into her heart like a filthy sewer. She was harsh and cruel, lecherous and drunken, headstrong and obstinate, eager to keep what she had got by theft, ready to spend where extravagance became dissolute, with no regard for trust and good faith, no concern for chastity. She rejected and spurned the divine powers, and in the place of our established religion worshipped with meaningless rituals some sacrilegious conception of a God whom she declared to be the "only God." She gave herself

[1]Text: LCL IX.14, p. 423.

to wine quite early in the morning, to adultery at all
hours. Everyone, including her husband, was quite
deceived.

From a very different perspective, the Christian Tertullian writes of the difficulties of a mixed marriage. He dis-
courages mixed marriages, which he thinks are likely to
compromise the Christian life. But from the hypothetical
situation he portrays, we can infer the kind of witness a
Christian woman in a heathen household might have to
make.

> 11.4.[2] Suppose she can perform the duties she owes her
> husband. Still, she will not be able to satisfy her Lord
> with a Christian way of life, since she will have beside her
> the servant of the devil, who, on behalf of his lord will
> take care to prevent the obligations and pursuits of the
> faithful. Thus, if a station is to be kept, her husband asks
> her to join him at the baths; if a fast is to be observed, her
> husband arranges a feast; if she ought to make a visit,
> never have household duties seemed more pressing. For
> who is likely to allow his own wife to go about through
> the low-class districts for the sake of visiting "brothers" in
> their homes? Who will easily give up his wife at night so
> she can attend, when necessary, a Christian meeting?
> Who will, with good feeling, endure her absence the
> whole night of the Easter festivities? Who, without suspi-
> cion, will send her on her way to the Lord's Supper, which
> they so grossly slander? Who will permit her to creep into
> prison to kiss the chains of a martyr? To greet a brother
> with a kiss? To wash the feet of saints? To give them food
> and drink, and care for them? If a brother should come
> from abroad, what hospitality will he find in a stranger's
> house? If the poor need aid, stores and provisions are
> closed against them.

There can be little doubt that Tertullian's scenario had
many counterparts, modified no doubt, in actual situations.

[2]Text: CCL 1.388.

Justin Martyr writing perhaps fifty years before Tertullian, describes the witness of one woman to her husband, and shows how her witness could reverberate far beyond her own household:

> 11.2[3] A certain woman lived with an undisciplined and licentious man; such was she too at one time. But when she had come to know the teachings of Christ, she began to practice self-control and endeavored to persuade her husband to the same good intent by recalling the teachings and presenting to him a message of punishment in everlasting fire upon those who would not live temperately and in accordance with "right reason." But he continued to indulge himself and alienated his wife by his actions. She, then, thinking it unholy to go to bed with a man who, against nature and against justice, tried every avenue of pleasure, wished to be freed from the bond of marriage. But her friends discouraged her, advising that she should continue to live with her husband in the hope that he would have a change of heart, so she forced herself to remain with him. But after he had gone off to Alexandria, she heard that his conduct was even worse, and so, in order not to have any part in his unrighteous and profane behavior by remaining both companion and bedfellow in their marriage, she gave him what you call a bill of divorce and left him. Now this fine fellow ought to have been pleased that his wife who had but a little while ago acted so unscrupulously with her servants and assistants, indulging in wine and every sort of evil, had now abandoned such behavior and wanted him to change his way of life, too. Instead, he resented her leaving him, and brought against her the charge that she was a Christian. And she presented a petition to you, the Emperor, thinking that she should be allowed to set her affairs in order first, and then defend herself against the charge.

Unable for the moment to prosecute his wife, the husband attacked the teacher Ptolemaeus, persuaded a centurion to

---

[3]Text: PG 6.444.

accuse him of being a Christian and to cast him into prison to await trial before Urbicus, prefect of Rome. On giving his witness, Ptolemaeus was condemned, whereupon a certain Lucius came forward to challenge Urbicus' judgment, was himself accused, made his confession, and was condemned. Still another came forward, and was also punished. One woman's witness in the confines of her home had eventually found its way to the center of Roman power. It is perhaps a token of the trustworthiness of the record that not a single conversion is recorded as a result of her life and words.

Two features of the story should be carefully noted. First, the silent witness of attitude and act was supported by the spoken word to her husband, a message whose contents Justin records. It was a message insisting on a pure and holy life, a message about Christ as a Teacher, and about a final judgment upon immoral living. Its strongly ethical character no doubt reflected the grievances the woman legitimately held against her husband, but we shall find nevertheless that its elements are central in the less personally motivated apologetic of early Christianity. Second, very little is said about the process of her own conversion, but Justin implies that she came to the faith through the guidance of a teacher, Ptolemaeus. We shall see in time how teachers, as catechists, came to play a crucial role in the presentation of the message and the conversion of pagans.

As a reliable account, Justin's narrative affords us a rare insight into the context in which many Christians witnessed to their faith by word and deed. Later legendary tales evoked a similar picture. In the *Acts of Xanthippe and Polyxena,* a romance whose *mise en scène* is a supposed mission of Paul to Spain, the domestic circle is broadened to include a slave. The slave, sent to Rome with letters from his master, happened to hear the word from Paul. Unable to stay sufficiently long in Rome to be instructed, he returned to Spain, beside himself with grief and longing. His changed attitude brought inquiry from his master; his reply was overheard by his mistress, Xanthippe, whose conscience was awakened. She sought eagerly for the light, finding it at last when Paul arrived in Spain. In this legend, Probus, the master, originally alienated because of his wife's continence, is eventually won to saving faith. The slave disappears from the story, but the vivid portrait at the beginning of the story does not allow us to forget his role as the initial mediator of the message.

A Christian's Witness in Society

Beyond the domestic circle Christians commonly found many opportunities to present the message of faith to their neighbors and companions. As in the stories above, changed attitudes, different mores, new values must have aroused the curiosity, and sometimes the anger, of pagan neighbors who would demand an explanation. Not least, Christians were marked by their reluctance to participate in public festivities, which they saw as demonic rituals of idolatry. Suspicion and resentment were aroused especially when the festivities from which the Christians withdrew were in honor of the Emperor. A famous passage in Tertullian's *Apology* hints at the powerful effect the Christian withdrawal from public celebrations had upon pagans:

> 35.1[4] For this reason, then, Christians are enemies of the people, because they pay to the Emperors neither empty nor false nor rash honors; because they celebrate their festivals as people of a true religion with discretion rather than indulgence. But what a fine service it is to bring hearth and couch into the open, to carouse throughout the streets, to turn the city into the appearance of a tavern, to become drunk, to rush in crowds to outrage, immorality and wanton pleasure. Is the common joy expressed by the common disgrace? Are those things appropriate to the festal days of princes which are not appropriate to other days? Those who observe propriety out of respect for Caesar will be the very ones who abandon it for the sake of Caesar; piety will be the

[4]Text: CCL 1.144.

licence to be immoral, while self-gratification will be counted as religion. Of course we ought to be condemned! For they wonder why we undertake prayers and festivities for Caesar when we are chaste and sober and decent. Why do we not on the festal day garland our doors with laurel, or challenge the daylight with lamps?

Martyrdom and the Message

Once aroused, the hostility, suspicion and fear felt by the pagans could well lead to a persecution which would offer the Christian a dramatic means of presenting, in word and deed, his message to the world. We must not underestimate the effect of Christian suffering upon the pagan mind. Tertullian's splendid image "The blood of martyrs is the seed of the Church" had already found expression, though with less formulaic power, in Justin Martyr's *Dialogue with Trypho*:

> 110...[5] Now it is evident that there is no one who terrifies and enslaves us who all over the world believe in Christ. For it is open to all to see that though we are beheaded, crucified, thrown to the lions, cast into prison and into the fire, and made to suffer every other kind of torture we do not abandon our confession. But the more we suffer these penalties, the more others become believers and worship God through the name of Jesus.

But Justin could speak not only in abstract terms; in personal experience he had felt the forceful argument inherent in the Christian's fearlessness before a martyr's death, and the message from that witness had struck home:

> 11.2[6] For I, too, while I was enjoying the teachings of Plato, heard the Christians slandered, but when I saw that they were fearless in the face of death and of everything else which is usually regarded as fearful, I consid-

[5]Text: PG 6.729.
[6]Text: PG 6.463. *The Acts of the Christian Martyrs.*

ered that they could not possibly be living in sin and devoted to pleasure. For would anyone who is a lover of pleasure, or licentious, and thinks it good to feast on human flesh, be able to welcome a death by which he will lose these "goods"? Would he not rather have tried in every way to continue his present life and escape the authorities; at least not betray himself, knowing he would die.

From two documents, both highly authentic, belonging to the earlier period of persecution, we are able to see how Christians seized the occasion of martyrdom to present the message. The first is an account of the trial of martyrs from Scilli, a town in North Africa whose exact location is still unknown. In content, it may be regarded as the official record of the proceedings, which took place on 17 July, 180. The trial apparently took place behind closed doors; the witness therefore had a limited audience.

[7]During the consulship of Claudianus and (for the second time) Praesens, on the 17th July at Carthage Speratus, Nartzalus and Cittinus, Donata, Secunda and Vestia were taken into the governor's inner court where the proceedings took place.

Saturninus the proconusl said: You can still receive the indulgence of our lord the Emperor if you return to your senses.

Speratus said: We have never done wrong, we have never abetted injustice; we have never uttered a curse on anyone, but have returned thanks when we have been unjustly treated. This we do out of respect for our Emperor.

Saturninus the proconsul said: We too are religious, but our religion is simple: we swear by the "genius" of our lord the Emperor and pray for his welfare, as you also should do.

[7]Text: OECT., ed. Musurillo, 86.

Speratus said: If you will listen quietly, I can explain the "hidden depths" of simplicity.

Saturninus said: I will not listen to you if you are going to slander our sacred rites. Rather, swear by the genius of our lord the Emperor.

Speratus said: I do not recognize the power of this world. But I serve rather the God whom no one has seen nor can see with these eyes of ours. I have never committed a theft; but whenever I buy, I pay the tax, because I know that my Lord is the King of kings and ruler over all the world.

Saturninus the proconsul then said to the others: Cease to be of this persuasion.

Speratus said: It is a bad persuasion to give false witness and to murder.

Saturninus the proconsul said: Abandon this madness.

Cittinus said: We fear no one except God our Lord who dwells in heaven.

Donata said: I honor Caesar as Caesar; but I fear God.

Vestia said: I am a Christian.

Secunda said: I am what I wish to be.

Saturninus the proconsul said to Speratus: Do you insist on being a Christian?

Speratus said: I am a Christian. —All affirmed that they were, too.

Saturninus the proconsul said: Do you not want some time to think it over?

Speratus said: There is no room for deliberation where the right cause is clear.

Saturninus the proconsul said: What is in your satchel?

Speratus said: The books and letters of Paul, a just man.

Saturninus the proconsul said: Take 30 days and reflect.

Speratus repeated: I am a Christian. —And all affirmed the same thing.

Saturninus the proconsul read his decision from a tablet: Speratus, Nartzalus, Cittinus, Donata, Vestia, Secunda and the rest have confessed that they live according to the Christian way of life. Since they stubbornly persist therein, in spite of the opportunity given to them to return to Roman ways, the judgment is that they die by the sword.

Speratus said: We give thanks to God.

Nartzalus said: Today in heaven we are witnesses: thanks be to God.

Saturninus the proconsul ordered that it should be proclaimed by a herald: Speratus, Nartzalus, Cittinus, Veturius, Felix, Aquilinus, Laetantius, Januaria, Generosa, Vestia, Donata and Secunda I have ordered to be executed.

They all cried: Thanks be to God.

Perhaps nothing in this account is more touching than the simplicity with which the martyrs, one after another, make their witness: "I am a Christian." Yet Speratus is willing to use the occasion to reveal the truth, to "explain the hidden depths of simplicity" to the proconsul, if he will listen. And in spite of the proconsul's refusal to hear, Speratus and Cittinus still find occasion to reveal the central elements of their faith: belief in the unseen God as ruler of all, high moral standards, and commitment to the welfare of society. Surprisingly, though they are on trial as Christians, the martyrs offer not a word about the centrality of Christ to Christian faith. As we proceed, we shall find on other occasions, too, an apparent reluctance to speak of Christ when Christians delivered the message to pagans.

In the second document, *The Passion of SS. Perpetua and Felicitas*, we are given a much fuller account of the sequence of events from the time of arrest to the death of the martyrs. Moreover, the central portion of the story is the actual diary of Perpetua who, as a well-educated woman of some social standing, was able to write. Her diary was edited with an introduction and conclusion added by a contemporary and evidently an eyewitness of her martyrdom. We thus have an authentic, highly personalized account with some striking details which suggest how and with what effect martyrdom offered a context for presenting the message. The martyrdom took place in Carthage on 7 March 203 (or possibly 202) as part of a celebration in honor of the birthday of Geta, the Emperor's son. The editor introduces the diary with a few important details:

> 2.[8]The young catechumens, Revocatus and his fellow-slave Felicitas, Saturninus and Secundulus were arrested. With them also was Vibia Perpetua, from the upper-class, well-educated, duly married. Both her father and mother were alive, and she had two brothers, one of whom was a catechumen like herself; she had as well a baby boy whom she was nursing. She was about twenty-two. She herself has told the story of her witness from this point on and has left it to us written by her own hand and from her own perspective.

The *Passion* reveals to us at least three distinct audiences to whom the martyrdom offered an occasion to witness. First, Perpetua's pagan father plays a rather pathetic role in the narrative. He repeatedly sought to dissuade her from her rash resolution, bringing deeply personal arguments to bear: the probable death of her infant son, and the disgrace to the family. Perpetua's response suggests that there had already been long discussions in the house about her faith—her father alone in the family still remained a devoted pagan—for her answers are short, somewhat cryptic, with a sense of finality; she is not explaining her faith to a stranger:

> 3. While we were still with the officials my father tried to persuade me with his words and to cast me down from

[8]Text: OECT., ed. Musurillo, 108-113.

the faith because of his love for me. "Father," I said, "Let
me take an example. Do you see this container lying here,
a water pot or something of the kind?" And he said, "Yes,
I see it." And I said to him, "Surely one cannot call it by
any name other than what it really is?" "No," said he. "So
also I cannot call myself anything but what I am—a
Christian. . . ."
5. After a few days, a report came that we should be
placed on trial. My father, however, arrived from the
town, weary and worn, and approached me to overturn
my faith, saying: "Take pity on my grey hairs, daughter.
Pity your father if such I may be called. . . " And I grieved
for the sad lot of my father since he alone of all my family
would not rejoice in my suffering. So I encouraged him,
and said, "Whatever God wills will happen before that
tribunal. Be assured that it is not we, but God who has the
power over our lives." And he departed, very sad.

A second audience to whom the martyrs witnessed were
the indeterminate and anonymous "crowds." In the *Passion*
the "crowds," however anonymous, take on a sort of corporate personality, curious, scornful, vindictive without a
cause. They evoke in the martyrs both fear and courage,
dismay and petulance—a reminder that the martyr's witness
could be a very human witness, indeed. The diary shows that
these crowds were present not only at the amphitheatre but
at several points in the process. We meet them, for example,
at the trial, for in contrast to the trial of the Scillitan
martyrs, this trial appears to have been held publicly.

6.[9] On another day while we were having breakfast, we
were suddenly taken away for a hearing. We reached the
forum. The report at once ran through the vicinity of the
forum and a huge crowd collected. We mounted the
platform. The others were interrogated and confessed.
When my turn came, my father appeared with my little
boy and drew me down a step saying: "Worship the gods.
Have pity on your child!" And Hilarian the procurator,

who then held the power of capital punishment in place of Minucius Timinianus, the recently deceased proconsul, said, "Spare your father's dignity! Spare your baby boy. Perform the sacrifice for the welfare of the Emperors." But I replied, "I cannot do it." Hilarian said, "Are you a Christian?" and I answered, "I am a Christian."

Following the judge's decision that Perpetua and her companions should be condemned to the wild beasts, the martyrs returned to the dungeon for sometime further. It was the custom, before the day of martyrdom, to give those about to die a "free meal." (Their needs had hitherto been cared for by the faithful who, often at the risk of their lives, brought food to the prison.) Here again, we learn that the dinner was set in a public place to satisfy the curious and the scornful, and to these the martyrs addressed (in a slightly petulant tone, it is worth noting) the Christian message of the Judgment. Their message apparently led to some conversions. At this point the editor continues the tale:

> 17.[10] On the day before their martyrdom when they came to their last meal, called the "free dinner," insofar as they could eat, they did not so much partake of a free meal as they enjoyed rather a "love feast." With firmness of purpose they cried out to the crowd, threatening the Judgment of God, affirming their felicity in suffering, mocking the curiosity of those who had gathered to watch. Thus Saturus said, "Is tomorrow not enough for you? Why do you look with such pleasure on what you hate? Friends today, enemies tomorrow! But mark well our faces, so that you may recognize them on the Judgment Day." With these words all were taken aback and departed, and many became believers.

In a moment, we shall see the crowd in the amphitheatre, thirsting for blood, yet with a dim and distorted glimmer of the significance of the martyr's act. But we must pause to note yet a third audience to whom the martyrs were able to

[10]Text: OECT, 124.

make a very personal appeal—the individual soldiers who became in some sense involved in their life in prison and their death in the arena. The assistant overseer of the prison recognizes the "great power" in them:

> 9.[11] Then after a few days a soldier, named Pudens, who was an officer's assistant and in charge of the prison, began to think highly of us, recognizing the great power within us, and to permit many to come to see us so that we might be refreshed and they in turn encouraged.

It was possibly the same Pudens who was guarding one of the entrances of the amphitheatre on the day of martyrdom, to whom Saturus spoke before he died. His words have a wistful ambiguity: do they suggest an incipient faith on the part of the soldier? Was the message already having its effect? Or are Saturus' words, and the ring dipped in his own blood, intended to be a message to the soldier, encouraging him by word and symbolic act to seek the significance of these events? It is here that the crowd emerges from the narrative once more, reflecting in their demonic chant a witness to the fact that the message of a martyr's death did not go unperceived.

> 21.[12] Likewise Saturus, at another gate, exhorted the soldier Pudens, saying, "It is exactly as I expected and predicted—not a single beast has yet attacked me. But now believe with your whole heart, for I am going forth and will perish by one bite of a leopard." And at once, when the show was almost finished, he was thrown to a leopard, and with one bite was covered with so much blood that as he was returning the crowd shouted the witness of his second baptism: "Bathed and saved! Bathed and saved!" For surely he was saved who had bathed in this manner. Then to the soldier Pudens he said, "Farewell, keep the faith in mind and remember me. Do not let these things disturb but rather strengthen

[11]Text: OECT, 116.
[12]Text: OECT, 128.

you." At the same time he asked Pudens for the ring on his finger; he dipped it in his blood and returned it to him as an heirloom, leaving him a token and a memorial of his blood. Then he lost consciousness and was cast with the rest into the place where they were usually dispatched.

It is clear that the narrative has placed relatively little emphasis on the content of the message of the martyrs insofar as it was spoken to these various audiences: a simple affirmation of faith to the father; to the crowds at the free dinner, a word about the Judgment; to the soldier a winsome appeal to reflect on the martyr's faith. At points the simple word had a telling effect, but the story gains its narrative power more from the deeds described than the message spoken, betraying perhaps the martyrs' conviction that it was in their deeds rather than their words that the strength of their message to the pagans lay.

A Christian's Witness in Secular Vocations

In calling attention to the myriad ways in which pagan social life evoked the witness of Christian faith, sometimes only with the message implied by a silent refusal to participate, I have made no specific mention of the challenges which came to Christians in the every day business of earning a living. In his work *On Idolatry* Tertullian shows how craftsman and merchant must say a firm "No" to all forms of money-making which entail idolatry. The implications, as Tertullian elaborates them, could be far reaching, and we shall not in general pursue them here. But one profession, that of the teacher, deserves special consideration. On the one hand, our most striking sources reflect little confidence that the pagan classroom could offer an opportunity to present the message; on the other, we have a witness in the Christian school of Origen at Caesarea to the powerful effect upon the pagan mind of an education under Christian auspices.

There were generally three levels of education in antiquity, basic education conducted by the *grammatistes* (also known in the Roman world as *ludi magister*), "middle" school at whose head was the *grammaticus* teaching grammar and literature, and the higher education of the *rhetor* who perfected the student's skills in writing and public speaking. It is probably to the first two types of teachers that Tertullian directs his admonition in *On Idolatry*. He does not see that the interpretation of a literary text provides an opportunity for the conscientious Christian to reveal the message of faith. On the contrary, "if the believer teaches literature, wherein one finds without question the praises of idols, he commends while he teaches, gives his assent to what he transmits, offers a witness to what he recalls (10.5)." Moreover, the structure and administration of the educational system is so bound up with idolatry that the only message a Christian can bring is that implied in his withdrawal from the system.

Almost two centuries later, Augustine expressed comparable reservations about the profession of the *rhetor*. In the first book of the *Confessions* he excoriates contemporary education for its false aims, perverse methods, and the ungodly content of its subject matter. He himself had gone through all its stages on the road to becoming finally a distinguished professor of rhetoric in the Imperial city of Milan. But after his conversion under Ambrose in 386 he felt constrained to give up his profession, for it was not one in which the witness to Christian truth could shine through the lies it was forced to tell:

> IX.2.[13] I decided in your sight, not indeed to break away suddenly, but to withdraw quietly from the use of my tongue in this "speech market." No longer should I sell weapons to arm the frenzy of young men, who were not so much interested in Your Law or Your peace as in the madness of lies and the battles of the law-courts.

[13]Text: LCL, ed. Watts, 11.4.

It is significant that some of Augustine's contemporaries seem to have found Augustine's bold act still not radical enough. A few lines further he tells us that they thought he should have abandoned at once his "Chair of Falsehood."

The Christian Schools of Antiquity

In spite of these strictures against popular education, the Church generally did not undertake to provide an equivalent educational system of its own. This is perhaps the more surprising in light of the experiment of the Catechetical School in Alexandria in the early third century. This school, under the leadership of several brilliant teachers, Pantaenus, Clement, and Origen, developed something like a Christian philosophy of education, in which literary and philosophical studies under Christian auspices could serve as a propaedeutic to theological studies. The school was evidently open to pagans and thus offered what must have appeared to its teachers as an ideal platform from which to present the message to them. When Origen fled to Caesarea in 233 he established a school on the model of the Alexandrian School, and in a eulogy delivered by Gregory the Wonder-Worker, a pagan who had been converted to Christianity in the course of his study at the school, we are given an extraordinarily detailed picture of how the message was presented there. The eulogy was delivered in the presence of his teacher as Gregory was about to "graduate," and we can assume therefore that if the picture is somewhat idealized, it is still in its outlines a creditable one.

It was rather by choice that Gregory found Origen's school. He had spent his youth in Neo-Caesarea (near the Black Sea) and was unexpectedly invited to accompany his sister to Antioch to join her husband who was in the service of the Roman governor of Syria. Eager to study law, he accepted the invitation because it offered an opportunity to visit the near-by Berytus with its distinguished school of law. Unexpectedly, he says, his journey carried him beyond Berytus to Caesarea. Here he met Origen whose subtle but compelling presentation of the message in the course of instruction won Gregory as a convert to the faith. Gregory recounts Origen's manner and methods in detail.

Gregory originally had no intention of staying a long time with Origen. But he found an overwhelming fascination with the speech and character of Origen who contrived every kind of argument to detain his newfound friend and induct him into his school.

> VI.80[14] He poured such a flood of words one after another over us that in the end we were like people bewitched, spellbound by his artless arts, and held by his words, in some marvellous way, with a sort of divine power. Then, too, he goaded us on with the stimulus of his friendship, which could not be easily disregarded, but was keen and effective, compounded of courtesy and a kind disposition, a sort of good will towards us affirmed in both his conversation and companionship. He did not try to talk circles around us to no purpose, but with an intent that was kind and sympathetic and directed to our advantage he wished to save us and to make us share in the pleasures of philosophy.

Once persuaded to stay with Origen, Gregory began the course of study. From his description, we gather that it was an effective sequential program, with a training first in dialectic with the intent of teaching a student "to think," so that one could "test opinions" and learn to distinguish the true from the false.

> VII.102[15] He taught us that this part of philosophy (dialectic) had many aspects and accustomed us to affirm and deny evidence not at random nor as anything came along, but only after careful examination...And he taught us not only to examine what was obvious and open to view, though such things are occasionally deceptive and fallacious, but to strip away the outward form

[14]Text: SC 148.126.
[15]Text: SC 148.138.

and penetrate to the interior of each subject. When we had determined that there was nothing unsound at the core, then we could have confidence in the inner structure and so come to a decision about matters on the surface. Thus he trained our minds to be critical of both language and words.

From dialectic, Origen led his students to science, and we can infer from Gregory's account the subtle questions, the silent intimations, wherein Origen raised expectations, set perspectives, which prepared his young audience for the message still to come:

> VIII.111[16] By the clarity of his teachings and arguments, some of which he learned from others, some of which he discovered for himself, about the sacred governance of the universe and the perfection of nature he brought our minds gradually, not to thoughtless amazement, but to reflective wonder. This is the lofty and inspired learning acquired by the investigation of nature, a science most delightful to all.

The curriculum also included ethics. In this school, the teaching of moral philosophy had as its aim not simply the acquisition of knowledge but the achievement of the good life. For this, Origen's own example proved to be of paramount importance:

> XI.135[17] He first exhorted us with his words to the study of philosophy, but his words were preceded by his deeds. He did not merely preach fine words. On the contrary, he was not satisfied to speak unless he followed his own precepts, striving with a sincere heart to practice what he preached. He tried himself to be the sort of person he described in his talk as living well, to be the model, I should like to say, of the wise man...This wonderful man, this friend and advocate of the virtues has long since made us the very keenest lovers, loving

[16]Text: SC 148.142.
[17]Text: SC 148.150.

what he perhaps alone possesses, inspiring us through his virtue with a love of the beauty of righteousness, whose golden face he has truly shown us.

The goal of the course of study was theology, and it was here that the message could be most fully presented. But Origen regarded philosophy as a useful preparation for theology, and his students therefore underwent a thorough training in the "History of Metaphysics." Origen's attitude was remarkably "liberal" though not without a carefully calculated bias: no opinion was to be rejected except that of the atheists. The atheists had nothing useful to say, but through the very disagreements of the rest Origen could warn the student not to be satisfied with any opinion until he had found indeed the true God:

> XIII.150[18] How could I go into the man's disposition and describe the preparation he wished us to have for learning the various views about the divine. He did not want us to fail on the most central matter of all—the knowledge of the cause of all things. He thought we should apply ourselves with the greatest energy to the study of philosophy by gathering up all the writings of the ancient philosophers and poets, and rejecting or refusing nothing, since we did not yet have the power to judge them. He excepted only the writings of the atheists who have lost all trace of human wisdom when they say there is neither God nor Providence. He did not think we should read these lest our mind should be sullied when it comes upon words opposed to the worship of God.

The coping-stone of the curriculum was theology, and it was as an exegete that Origen was most inspiring; the love in his own soul for the Bible kindled a fire in the hearts of his students. Gregory praises his skill in expounding the dark sayings of Scripture. The Divine Word, the Leader of men, says Gregory,

[18]Text: SC 148.158.

XV.176[19] The Prince of all, who speaks through the prophets beloved of God and bestows all prophecy, all mystic and divine speech, has honored this man as a friend, making him the interpreter of his oracles. Through this man he has brought to light what he spoke only in riddles through others. Things which he who is worthy of all trust either commanded as a king or simply announced, he gave to this man the ability to search out and discover their intent. Whether one was stubborn and skeptical or eager to learn, if he were taught by this man he would be somehow compelled to understand, and to choose to believe and to follow God.

As a brilliant and inspirational teacher, Origen was able to project the message as much by force of character as by word of mouth. He understood the persuasive power of a curriculum appropriately designed, of the subtle hint and the provocative question, of the personal example, of love for and sympathy with young minds. In Origen the teacher, medium and message were inseparable.

We set out in this chapter to discover the many informal, sometimes incidental, ways in which Christians in their daily lives might present the message of Christian faith to their families, their neighbors, and to society at large. It seemed appropriate, in the context of our discussion about the Christian's witness in his professional career, to include a portrait of Origen's school at Caesarea. The witness of this school was, as we have just seen, more than incidental: it seems to have been a well-designed attempt to present the message within an educational system. We have thus anticipated the main direction this study must take: the discovery of those explicit efforts made by Christians to present the message with a more deliberate eye to form and content. We shall look first at the Church's message to the Jews.

[19]Text: SC 148.168.

Suggestions for Further Reading

Barnes, Timothy D., *Tertullian. A Literary and Historical Study*. Oxford 1971.

Chapter 7 contains a cautious account of the means by which the Christian message was spread in the great centers of the Empire; chapter 11 assesses the roles played by emperor, governors and the populace in the persecutions of the Christians.

Benko, Stephen and John J. O'Rourke, *The Catacombs and The Colosseum. The Roman Empire as the Setting of Primitive Christianity*. Valley Forge 1971.

A collection of essays by various authors describing "the social and political forces which affected the development of the early Christian Church." Two chapters are of special importance for our study: chapter 6 "Ancient Education in the time of the early Roman Empire" (John J. Townsend), and chapter 12 "Collegia, Philosophical Schools, and Theology" (Robert L. Wilkin). The latter shows how the early Christian message responded to pagan perceptions of Christian society.

Frend, W.H.C., *Martyrdom and Persecution in the Early Church*. New York 1967.

A detailed account of the persecutions of the first three centuries of our era.

Latourette, Kenneth S., *A History of the Expansion of Christianity. Vol. 1: The First Three Centuries*. New York 1937.

Chapter 4 describes the methods used in the early centuries to present the message whether by itinerant missionaries or by the common Christian in his everyday life.

Musurillo, H.A. (ed. tr.), *The Acts of the Christian Martyrs.* Oxford 1972.

The introduction discusses in each case the difficult question of authenticity.

Chapter Two

THE MESSAGE TO THE JEWS

A basic pattern for the witness of early Christianity to both Jew and Gentile had been sharply outlined in the New Testament. As the Gentile world rapidly became much the larger field for missionary activity, Christians developed a variety of methods and forms for the presentation of the message, which if rooted in the Biblical pattern, went far beyond it shaping it to suit the needs of their particular audiences. In the case of the Jewish audience, on the other hand, our evidence suggests that the Church maintained a somewhat firmer adherence to the models presented in the New Testament, though one can see developments here too.

The sermons of Peter and Paul in *Acts* offer a striking witness to the tenor of the earliest Christian message to the Jews. Peter's sermon on Pentecost (Acts 2:14-40) shows that at the heart of the earliest kerygma, or message, was the narration of the suffering, death, resurrection and exaltation of Christ, with a call to repentance. We must note in addition his stress on Christ as the descendant of David, and the fulfillment of prophecy, particularly in the promises made to David. There is a winsome simplicity in the logic by which the Apostle appeals to facts: the Scripture which promises that "thy Holy One will not see corruption" cannot apply to David for David as a matter of fact is dead;

therefore it applies to Christ. We also note that in this earliest sermon there is only the slightest implication of guilt on the part of the Jews: "This Jesus, delivered up according to the definite plan and foreknowledge of God, you crucified and killed by the hands of lawless men" (2:23).

In his second sermon, on the Temple Porch (Acts 3:12-26), Peter again proclaims the suffering, death, resurrection and exaltation of Jesus as the fulfillment of prophecy. But the implication of Jewish guilt is more obvious: "... You delivered up and denied (Jesus) in the presence of Pilate, when he had decided to release him. But you denied the Holy and Righteous One, and asked for a murderer to be granted to you, and killed the Author of Life, whom God raised from the dead" (3:13, 14).

Our first view in Acts of Paul's message to the Jews comes from his "exhortation" in the synagogue at Antioch of Pisidia (Acts 13:16-41). Like Peter he stresses the suffering, death, resurrection and exaltation of Christ with an appeal to repentance. He, too, places Christ in the line of David. But we also find the central kerygmatic events set in the context not only of prophecy, but of a narrative of Hebrew history. This narrative not only places Christ at the culminating point of Hebrew history, but also serves to remind his listeners, however gently, that the Jews have been from the beginning a rebellious people: for forty years God "bore with them in the wilderness" (13:18); though God gave them judges, "they asked for a king" (13:21). Paul further points to the blindness of the Jews in a tone which hints at its unaccountability: "For those who live in Jerusalem and their rulers, because they did not recognize him nor understand the utterances of the prophets which are read every sabbath, fulfilled these by condemning him. Though they could charge him with nothing deserving death, yet they asked Pilate to have him killed" (13:27-8). It is worth noting, that the appeal to history to demonstrate that the Jews were a "stiff-necked people," always "resisting the Holy Spirit" (Acts 7:51) had had a notable precedent in Stephen's speech to the Jews at his martyrdom, which, according to the author of Acts, Paul witnessed (7:58).

We can find a thematic parallel to these early Apostolic sermons in the dialogue of the risen Lord with two Jews on the road to Emmaus (Lk 24:13-25). The Evangelist puts into the mouth of the Jews the narrative, central, as we have seen, to the kerygma, of the crucifixion and resurrection of Jesus of Nazareth. It is Christ himself who disputes with these Jews, showing how Moses and the prophets speak of the suffering and exaltation of Christ, "opening" to them the Scriptures. Christ also expresses amazement at their blindness: "O foolish men, and slow of heart to believe all that the prophets have spoken!" (24:25). But the story has a happy sequel: in the eating of the bread "their eyes were opened ...and he vanished out of their sight" (24:31).

Throughout these accounts some well-defined themes emerge as characteristic of the message to the Jews: that the Jesus who suffered and died is shown by his resurrection and exaltation to be the true descendant of David and the "Holy One" of God; that these events are spoken of in the Scriptures, and are indeed the fulfillment of Old Testament History; that the Jews are strangely blinded, but that the time has come to repent.

We shall return presently to trace further the development of themes in the message to the Jews, but we should observe in passing some New Testament evidence for the form and manner of presenting the message at the most primitive stage. Luke's account, in which our Lord is participant, may appear to give a certain primacy to the dialogue form. In the early Apostolic ministry on the other hand, we find evidence, not so much of the dialogue, as of its more formal and intense counterpart, the public debate or disputation. In the passages considered above from the Book of Acts, the context for the presentation of the message is Temple, Council and Synagogue, all of which called for a fairly formal sermon, address, or exhortation. But in chapters 17-19 the author of Acts portrays Paul as moving from city to city throughout Greece, entering first the synagogue to argue, dispute or preach to the Jews. Paul's activity is designated by the Greek verb *dialegeisthai* in Acts 17:2; 17:17; 18:4; 18:19; 19:8; and 19:9. Ernst Haenchen has shown in his Commentary on Acts (trans R. Mcl. Wilson, 1971) that while in some cases the verb must mean "to preach," in other cases it must suggest rather disputation and debate, possibly a lecture followed by a discussion. The account of Apollos in Acts 18:24-28 is relevant here. A native of Alexandria, he went to Ephesus and while there spoke boldly in the synagogue about Jesus, "though he knew only the baptism of John." He was consequently better instructed by Priscilla and Aquila, and then made his way to Greece. "When he arrived, he greatly helped those who through grace had believed, for he powerfully confuted the Jews in public, showing by the Scriptures that the Christ was Jesus." The verb *diakatelegcheto* (confuted) may well imply cross-examination, hence here public disputations with the Jews.

The point has some importance, because, if we are correct, we can trace an early Christian tradition going back to the New Testament, of public disputations between Christians and Jews. We must, of course, assume that with time came changes in the character, possibly even, in the motivation of the disputations. They would not necessarily be held in the synagogues, and sheer desire for victory in debate must often have been present. Yet in all likelihood Christians would regard them as means of presenting the message, and perhaps hope that an audience at least partially Jewish could be reached in this way. Two brief accounts of such disputations demand our attention.

Origen, writing just before 250 A.D. against Celsus, a pagan opponent whom we shall meet again, recalls a disputation he himself had with some Jews:

> 1.45[1]I remember that I once employed the following argument in a debate with some Jewish "wise men" in the presence of many judges. "I should like you to answer a question, gentlemen. History records that there have been two men who have lived with the human race and performed wonderful deeds beyond the power of man.

[1]Text: SC 132.192.

One of these is Moses, your lawgiver, who wrote about himself, the other is Jesus, our Teacher, who left no memoirs of his own, but his disciples have borne witness to him in the Gospels. On what grounds do you believe Moses to be trustworthy, though the Egyptians accused him of being a sorcerer and a juggler, but you disbelieve Jesus, whom you accuse? For both have their witnesses: the Jews affirm Moses, while the Christians—who do not deny the power of prophecy given to Moses but even deduce therefrom the truth of the narratives about Jesus—receive as true the strange things written about the latter by his disciples. Now if you ask us for proof about Jesus, then first give us proof about Moses, his predecessor. But if you hesitate and avoid a demonstration concerning Moses who came first, for the present we too will refuse to give our evidence.

Origen describes the setting here with tantalizing brevity; even so we can gather a somewhat impressionistic picture of at least one Christian scholar (there might well have been others) opposed to learned Jews (Rabbis?) with a considerable audience who acted as judges. The manner and tone of the Christian argument also arrests our attention: a somewhat impatient insistence on comparable evidence for comparable claims, and the threat of a curt dismissal of the question unless the Jews cooperate. One recognizes, of course, a model for the *form* of this argument (you reply to my question before I reply to yours) in Jesus' answer to the Jews who questioned his authority (see Mark 11:27-33 and parallels), but Origen's petulance is a rather far cry from the authoritative confidence of Jesus.

Tertullian, Against the Jews

A generation earlier (shortly after 200 A.D.) Tertullian tells of a debate between a Christian and a Jewish proselyte. His narrative like that of Origen, offers a fleeting glimpse of the setting, in particular, the unruly audience, and the con-

fusion of the debate itself; while Tertullian thinks it worth
noting that Jewish proselytes were as eager to debate as
native Jews:

> 1.[2] There occurred recently a debate between a Chris-
> tian and a Jewish proselyte. They tugged back and forth
> on their line of argument until evening. On each side were
> bystanders clamoring support and the truth was over-
> shadowed by a cloud. I wished therefore to consider more
> carefully and to complete in a written treatise the ques-
> tions discussed there where they could not be fully eluci-
> dated due to the conditions of the debate. For an
> opportunity for defending the divine grace bestowed
> upon the gentiles acquires importance from the fact that
> the man who undertook to defend the Law was himself a
> Gentile and not a Jew from the stock of Israel.

Since Tertullian's work appears to be a clarification of the
points made at the disputation, we must pause to investigate
its fundamental themes. Unfortunately, we do not know
how much of the debate is represented in this treatise since
the latter part (chapters 9-14) is an addition, probably by
another hand, with material gathered from Book III of
Tertullian's treatise *Against Marcion*. In chapters 1-8, however, the message is drawn in sharp outline. I list below its
four major themes, and illustrate the argument with abbre-
viated paraphrases from the text:

1) *God promised that the Gentiles would find God's grace
   and become superior to the Jews who have always been
   idolaters at heart.*

> 1.3...[3] God told Rebecca that two nations were in her
> womb one of whom would overcome the other, the
> "greater" serving the "lesser" [Gen 25:23]. Now Jews may
> be regarded as "greater" than Christians both because as
> a people they preceded the Christians, and because in the
> Law they are God's favored people. To fulfill the Scrip-

[2]Text: CCL 2.1339.
[3]Text: CCL 2.1340.

ture, then, the Jews or the "greater" people must serve the Christians, and the Christians, the "lesser" people, must overcome the Jews. For Scripture reveals how the Jews forsook God to serve idols thus losing the favor of God, while the Christians have forsaken idols to serve God, gaining His favor. This is why the lesser people have overcome the greater.

2) *God's law is "natural law," constantly in the process of reformulation to suit the needs of specific peoples in specific circumstances.*

> 11.9.[4] We understand that the law of God existed before Moses...first, indeed, in Paradise and later among the Patriarchs. Even for the Jews it has been reshaped at certain times. For the Gentiles God revealed a law subsequent to that of Moses, a new and better law promised by the prophets, and he declared that the law of Moses given for a limited time should be kept for a limited time. We must not take from God this power to reformulate the law in accordance with the needs of the time and with a view to our salvation.

3) *Circumcision was given for a sign to mark the Jews as those whom God had rejected and punished by Titus' destruction of Jerusalem and Hadrian's prohibition against Jews entering the city.*

> 111.4.[5] Circumcision therefore was given for a sign by which in recent times Israel could be recognized when, as they deserved, they were prevented from entering the holy city. As the prophet says: "Your land shall be deserted, your cities burned with fire, and aliens will consume the wealth of your land in your very presence" [Is 1:7-8]...For this reason the prophet later reproached them: "I begot sons and honored them, but they have spurned me" [Is 1:2]...Thus they are now prevented from entering Jerusalem.

[4]Text: CCL 2.1343.
[5]Text: CCL 2.1345.

4) *The Christ has come is proven by the fulfillment of the prophecy that all nations will worship Him.*

> VII.6...[6] For who would have been able to rule over all except Christ? Whom did the Scriptures announce as about to reign over all the nations forever?... The name and rule of Christ extends everywhere, everywhere he reigns. With him neither king nor commoner finds greater esteem. He is the same to all, king over all, judge of all, God and Lord of all. Can you hesitate to believe what is happening before your very eyes?

The harsh attitude to the Jews represented here emerges from a line of thought which, as we have seen, was already developing in the Book of Acts. But the "message" of this treatise goes further than the sermons in Acts in its attempt to explain the Mosaic law in terms both of natural law and salvific history, and its attempt to understand the relation of two peoples, Jews and Gentiles, from the point of view of the Divine plan. In these, we recognize more than a century of Christian reflection on Paul's Epistle to the Romans. At the same time, we cannot fail to note the malicious advantage taken of historical circumstances to explain circumcision and to tie it to the traditional theme of Israel's guilt and consequent rejection by God, a theme expressed in the New Testament, not with malice, but with pain and amazement.

Justin Martyr, Dialogue with Trypho

Tertullian's message to the Jews was, in part at least, already embodied in a work written a half-century earlier (between 160 and 165) by Justin Martyr, the *Dialogue with Trypho the Jew.* This work, as its title suggests, reflects not a public disputation, but a private conversation in the midst of friends. While we may believe that Origen and Tertullian have left us a fairly faithful record of the events they describe, scholars are uncertain how accurately Justin's

[6]Text: CCL 2.155.

Dialogue portrays an actual event. The consensus is that though the *Dialogue* may indeed grow out of a historical conversion, as we have it, it is highly fictitious. If so, the *Dialogue* as a form for presenting the message gains importance, for the author has deliberately brought the intentionality of art to the elucidation of an actual event. The form therefore has significance for our investigation.

We may suggest first that if the *Dialogue* reflects an actual conversation, the event achieves by its artistic representation the authority of a model. Christian dialogue with Jews is not merely something that happened, but something which should be made to happen; it is an appropriate way to present the message. It is possible that Justin understood the advantages of the dialogue over the public disputation: it is more congenial, more conducive to mutual respect, less open to the arrogance and showmanship which so easily arise in the presence of an audience. Indeed, Justin insists on cordiality as the condition of discussion. When some of Trypho's friends jeer at Justin's words, he objects:

> 9.[7] Once again those who were with Trypho laughed and shouted insults. Then I got up as though I intended to leave. But he caught my cloak and said I should not depart until I had fulfilled my promise. "Do not, then" I said, "permit your companions to raise such a clamor and to act in such a disrespectful way. If they wish, they can listen in silence; if more important concerns press upon them, they can go away. But as for you and me, let us withdraw and rest and there finish our discussion." Trypho approved, and so we turned and came to the middle of the Xystus. Two of his companions scoffed and mocked our zeal, then departed. But when we had come to the place where there were stone seats on either side, Trypho and his companions who had remained sat on the one side, and we again took up the conversation.

Second, it seems probable that Justin deliberately incorporated elements into his dialogue which would recall the

[7]Text: PG 6.493C.

conversation of Christ with two Jews on the road to Emmaus and thereby give an undeniable authentication to the form of his message. There are, to be sure, great differences in the Lukan narrative and Justin's *Dialogue*. But two features are suggestive:

1) Justin makes a persistent effort to "open the Scripture" to Trypho, showing how the life and saving work of Christ and the growth of the Church is "contained" in the Old Testament. This is a matter of principle for when Justin asserts that there are allusions to Christ as God in the Old Testament, Trypho says:

> 56.[8] Prove your point. For as you see evening approaches and we are not prepared to undertake a reply in such precarious matters since we have never heard anyone discuss these things whether in exploration or demonstration. And we would not have put up with you in your exposition had you not referred every point to the Scriptures. You are eager to establish your case from them.

2) The dialogue ends, not, admittedly, with the conversion of Trypho, but a recognition that, for his part, much had been learned. Justin departs, for he must set sail. We do not have a resolution here, but there is a parallel with Justin's own conversion recounted in chapters 2-7, where a man having led him to the Scriptures, departed, not to be seen again.

> 8.[9] At once a fire was lit in my soul and a passion seized me for the prophets and for those men who are the friends of Christ. Reflecting upon his (the man's) words, I found that this philosophy alone was useful and secure.

The opening of the Scriptures, the sudden disappearance of the man of God, the burning heart, all recall the Lukan account. Justin disappears before Trypho's heart is

---

[8]Text: PG 6.601C.
[9]Text: PG 6.492C.

inflamed, but the parallels in the two accounts hint that this, too, will follow for Trypho, as it had for Justin. Thus the *Dialogue*, with its model in our Lord's post-resurrection appearance, is to be understood as an effective and authoritative form in which to present the message.

Finally, Justin accents the authority of the Dialogue form by placing, as we have just seen, a dialogue within a dialogue. Justin's own conversion took place as a result of a dialogue, but through a rather different path of conversation. Justin was a Syrian, with a Greek education and had turned from one philosophy to another seeking spiritual satisfaction. At last he discovered the Platonists. One day when he was taking a solitary walk rapt in contemplation "an old man of distinguished appearance, and a manner gentle and holy" met him and began to interrogate him with Platonist dialectic:

> 3.[10] "Are you then," he said, "a lover of words but not at all a lover of deeds or of truth? Do you not try to be a man of action, but only a man of reflection and words?"
>
> "But what greater good ought one do," I said, "than to demonstrate by means of words the 'reason' which underlies and controls all things? or to grasp that reason and to be supported by it and so to see clearly how others, in their wanderings and pursuits, do nothing wholesome, nothing dear to God? Without philosophy and 'right reason' there can be no wisdom. Hence it is necessary that everyone be a philosopher, and to regard this the greatest and noblest deed, and all other things quite secondary, unless indeed they are related to philosophy which gives them some value and makes them worthy to be sought. But if they are without philosophy, if philosophy is not present, then they become ignoble and burdensome to those who pursue them."
>
> "Does philosophy bring happiness?" he said, interrupting me.
>
> "Yes, indeed, and it alone," I replied.

[10]Text: PG 6.480B.

"Tell me if you can," he said, "what is philosophy and what is the happiness it brings?"

"Philosophy is the understanding of 'Being' and the knowledge of truth. Happiness is the reward of this understanding and of wisdom."

"Well, then, what do you say God is?" said he.

Through Platonist dialectic, the old man shows Justin only that he cannot find his way to God by unaided rational speculation, and he offers a new path:

7.[11] "What teacher then should one employ," I said, "or how is one to find help, if philosophers do not have the truth?"

"Long ago—long before these so-called philosophers—there lived some men who were just and happy and beloved by God. Speaking through the divine Spirit they foretold events which would come to pass, and which indeed are now occurring. They are called 'prophets.' These alone both saw and spoke the truth to men, without reservation, without fear of anyone, caring nothing for glory; filled with the Holy Spirit, they spoke only what they heard and saw. Their writings even now remain and anyone who has turned to them in trust has received enormous help on questions of the source and goal of existence and on philosophical problems in general. For their discourse was not with logical demonstration, since as faithful witnesses of the truth they transcended all scientific proof. The course of events in the past and the present compel assent to their words. Moreover they have justly acquired the confidence of others because of the mighty deeds which they performed. They both glorified the maker of all as God and Father, and preached that Christ his Son should come from him. This the false prophets who were filled with an unclean and guileful spirit never did nor do now. Rather, they dare to work miracles for the astonishment of men,

[11]Text: PG 6.492A.

and thus honor demons and spirits of error. Above all
else, pray that the gates of light be opened to you, for
these things cannot be seen or understood unless God and
his Christ grant you understanding.

It cannot be unintended that this dialogue, so interesting
as an account of the way in which the message was convinc-
ingly presented to a Gentile, should serve almost as a fron-
tispiece for a Dialogue with the Jew. If, on the one hand, it
affirms the dialogue as an ideal form of Christian witness
whether to Jew or Gentile, it appears to make on the other, a
distinction between dialogue as dialectic (the invention of
the Greeks) and the dialogue as "opening the Scriptures"
(the model of the risen Christ). It is the latter that Justin will
use in presenting the message to Trypho.

In theme, Justin's message shows both continuity with
and development from the speeches in Acts. At the heart of
Justin's message lie the facts of the suffering and risen
Christ, and it is this which Trypho wishes to make central,
just as the apostles undertook to do in the Book of Acts. But
the Apostolic efforts in Acts to prove that Jesus as the Christ
is also the "Holy One of God" have their counterpart in
Justin, and with a significant theological development:
Christ is not only the Holy One; he is also the preexistent
Son of the Father! Justin knows that some Christians prefer
to think that Jesus became the Christ by "election," and
possibly for that reason emphatically insists on demonstrating the preexistence of Christ. When Justin digresses to
affirm that he will communicate with Judaizing Christians,
but only if they do not insist on all Christians keeping the
Law, Trypho brings him back to the major issue:

48.[12] And Trypho said, "I have heard your opinions on
these matters. Now continue the argument where you left
it, for it seems highly unlikely and by no means capable of
proof. For to say that this Christ existed as God before
time and then was willing to become man, but that he is

___
[12]Text: PG 6.580A.

not a man from men, strikes me as paradoxical, even ridiculous."

To this I replied: "I realize the account must seem paradoxical, especially to people of your race who have never been willing to understand or to do the things of God, but only to follow your own teachers, as God himself laments. Still, it will not destroy my fundamental point that he is the Christ of God even if I should not be able to demonstrate that a Son of the Creator of the world preexisted as God and became man by being born of a virgin. Hence, since I have satisfactorily demonstrated that whatever he may be, this is the Christ of God, even if I do not demonstrate his preexistence, or that he assumed flesh and experienced our humanity according to the will of the Father, it is fair to say that in this alone am I wrong, and not to deny that he is the Christ at least on the terms that he appeared as a man, born of men, and was shown to be the one chosen for the Christ. For, friends, some of our own people confess that this is the Christ, but say that he is merely a man born of men. With these I do not agree, nor would the majority of our people who think as I do. For we have been commanded by the Christ himself to believe not the teachings of men, but what was announced by the blessed prophets and taught by him.

For Justin, the humiliation of Christ is not merely the shameful suffering of God's "chosen" man upon a cross, but the assumption of manhood on the part of God.

Justin's message also goes beyond the speeches in Acts in describing *how* Christ's birth and death are redemptive. We can begin to see at this point the enormous influence of Paul's epistle to the Romans in the developing message to the Jews. Just as Paul in Romans 5 went beyond the history of Israel to Adam and the fall of man to establish the universal significance of the work of Christ, so Justin presents both the virgin birth and the death of Christ as a reversal of man's first sin. In a striking paragraph, he sets the virgin birth in the context of the preexistence of Christ:

100.[13] He gave the name "Peter" to one of his disciples who had formerly been known as Simon since through a revelation from the Father he had recognized him to be the Christ, the Son of God. And since we have it written in the memoirs of his apostles that he is the Son of God, and since we call him "Son" we understand that by the power and will of the Father before all creation he came forth—who is addressed also in the writings of the prophets variously as Wisdom, Day, Dawn, Sword, Stone, Staff, Jacob, Israel. He became a man through the Virgin so that the means by which transgression arose might be the same means by which it would come to an end. For Eve was a virgin, untouched, but, impregnated with the word of a snake, she brought forth disobedience and death. The Virgin Mary, however, was filled with faith and joy when the Angel Gabriel announced to her that the Spirit of the Lord would come upon her, the power of the Highest overshadow her, and the Holy Child born of her would be the Son of God; and she replied, "May it be to me according to your word" [Lk 1: 38]. Of her has he been born about whom so many Scriptures speak, as we have shown, and through whom God overthrows the snake, and those angels and men who are like it. But he brings deliverance from death to those who repent of their evil and believe on him.

Of Christ's death on the Cross he says:

94.[14] Tell me, was it not God who commanded through Moses that neither image nor likeness of anything in the heavens above or on the earth should be made; yet He himself through Moses had a bronze serpent made and erected for a sign through which those bitten by the snakes were healed. Surely He is not guilty of sin! Through this he proclaimed, as I said before, a mystery by which he announced that he would destroy the power of the serpent which had caused Adam's transgression.

[13]Text: PG 6.709C.
[14]Text: PG 6.700A.

To those, however, who believe upon him, the Crucified One, of which the bronze serpent was the "sign," there would be salvation from the serpent's bites, which are evil deeds, idolatry and other unrighteous acts. If you cannot accept this, give me a good reason why he set up the bronze serpent of Moses for a sign, and ordered those bitten to look upon it, with the result that they were healed, even though he had earlier commanded that no one make a likeness of any kind.

The influence of Pauline theology can also be felt in Justin's efforts to find a place for the Law in history. It is perhaps regrettable that Justin's solution has little of the positive affirmation of Paul, or indeed of the historical coherence of Tertullian. Following Paul, Justin assumed a "natural law" valid for all men; Justin also believed as Tertullian would later demonstrate, that the natural law was prior to the Mosaic Law, and was universally binding. The Jews received a special law because they were a particularly stubborn and rebellious people, and only by the constant reminder of precepts could they keep God before them. To Trypho he says:

46.[15] You should understand that God through Moses enjoined all these commandments upon you because of your people's hardness of heart, so that by the very multitude of these you might always keep God in mind in your every deed and not begin to be unjust to your neighbor or irreverent toward God.

This theme becomes almost a refrain in his message, particularly where he undertakes to explain the Law:

20.[16] For God enjoined you to abstain from certain foods so that you might have God in mind in your eating and drinking, since you are prone and ready to depart from the knowledge of him.

[15]Text: PG 6.576A.
[16]Text: PG 6.517B.

> 21.[17] God commanded you to keep the Sabbath, as I
> said before, for a sign, because of both your own unright-
> eousness and that of your fathers, and for the same
> reason imposed many other rules upon you.

But Justin offers us no hint of the large place of the Jews,
as seen by Paul in Romans, in the cosmic purposes of a
beneficent God. Although he recognizes that individuals
among them can be saved on the same basis as Gentiles, that
is, through faith in Christ, he insists that as a people they
have been completely rejected. Like his apostolic predecessors, Justin sees the rejection of the Jews as the punishment
for their perpetual hostility to God, a hostility demonstrated
by the fact that they "have slain the Just One and His
prophets before Him," but also by the fact that they are the
instigators of the persecution against the Christians, a point
in which he goes beyond the Apostolic word:

> 17.[18] You have done more than the Gentiles to bring
> harm upon us and upon Christ, since you are responsible
> for the false prejudice they harbor against the Just man
> and against us, his followers. For not only did you crucify
> that man who alone was blameless and just, by whose
> wounds those who come to the Father through him may
> be healed, but after you knew he had risen from the dead
> and ascended into heaven as the prophets predicted, not
> only did you not repent of the evil you had done, but you
> selected special agents from Jerusalem and sent them into
> all the world to say that the godless heresy of the Chris-
> tians had arisen, and to recount all the stories which those
> tell who are ignorant of us. Thus you are responsible not
> only for your own wickedness but for that of all others as
> well.

Indeed, Justin goes even further, and anticipates Tertullian's view that circumcision was given as a sign to mark those
who, since Hadrian's repression of Bar Kokhba's revolt in
135, could no longer return to the Holy City:

[17]Text: PG 6.520B.
[18]Text: PG 6.512B.

16.[19] For the circumcision according to the flesh which is from Abraham, was given for a sign; that you may be separated from the other nations and from us; and that you alone may suffer that which you now justly suffer; and that your land may be desolate, and your cities burned with fire; and that strangers may eat your fruit in your presence, and not one of you may go up to Jerusalem.

But the rejection of the Jews has only served to put into a clearer light God's alternate plan. For it is not the Jews, but the Christians who are and, in his grand design, always have been God's chosen people:

119.[20] After that just man had been slain we blossomed forth as another people flourishing like young and healthy sprouts as the prophets said: "Many nations shall flee to the Lord in that day and form a people, and they shall dwell in the midst of the whole earth" [Zech 2:11]. But we are not only a people, but a holy people as well, as I have already shown: "And they shall call it a holy people, redeemed by the Lord" [Is 62:12]. We are not therefore a vulgar crowd of common folk, nor a barbarian tribe, nor a people like the Carians and Phrygians, but God has chosen us and he has been revealed to those who did not seek Him: "Behold," he says, "I am God to a people which did not call upon my name" [Is 55:5]. For this is that people which God long ago promised to Abraham, when he declared that he would make him a father of many nations.

The affirmation that Christians rather than Jews are the people of God may be regarded as the thematic goal of the *Dialogue*, for it is a predominant theme in the concluding chapters. Yet it must not escape our notice that, even so, Christ and the Church are seen more as the fulfillment of prophecy than as the fulfillment of history. In his message to

[19]Text: PG 6.509A.
[20]Text: PG 6.752B.

Trypho, Justin failed to see the significance of the historical problem on which Paul reflected in Romans, and to which Tertullian would sketch an answer in his treatise *Against the Jews.*

The form of dialogue and debate, the proclamation of the Messiah, the appeal to Scripture, the characterization of the Jews as stubborn, their consequent rejection by God—all these reflect the abiding influence of the earliest message to the Jews. Within the framework, we can see efforts at elaboration, growing out of both the Church's developing theological sensitivity and the special interests of individuals. Justin, the one-time Platonist, would like to include in his message a Christian metaphysic about the relation of the Father and Son, though he recognizes that this is not absolutely essential to the message. Tertullian, with a strong historical sense, works out along lines already sketched by Paul the significance of Jewish history. From a modern point of view the interpretation of history would seem to form more suitable bridges between Christian and Jew. We can hear—and understand—the choke in Trypho's throat when he learns that he has not only a historical hurdle to jump, but a metaphysical one as well!

Suggestions for Further Reading

Barnard, L.W., *Justin Martyr. His Life and Thought.* Cambridge 1966.

A general study. Chapter 4 attempts to demonstrate the Hellenistic-Jewish milieu of the *Dialogue with Trypho* and Justin's efforts to shape his message to that milieu.

Daniélou, J., *The Origins of Latin Christianity.* Trans. David Smith and J.A. Baker. London and Philadelphia 1977.

Shows how anti-Jewish polemic helped to shape Latin Christianity, with several chapters devoted to early Christian dialogue with Jews.

Dodd, C.H., *The Apostolic Preaching and its Development.* New York 1964.

An attempt to recover from the New Testament evidence the fundamental form of the earliest Christian message.

de Lange, N.R.M., *Origen and The Jews. Studies in Jewish Christian Relations in Third Century Palestine.* Cambridge 1976.

Chapters 7 and 8 collect the evidence available in Origen for the debates between Christians and Jews.

McDonald, James I.H., *Kerygma and Didache. The Articulation and Structure of the Early Christian Message.* Cambridge 1980.

The book attempts to define and describe four forms which the earliest Christian message assumed: prophecy, preaching, teaching, and tradition.

Chapter Three

THE MESSAGE TO
THE PAGANS I

I

It is one of the major aims of the Book of Acts to portray the movement of the Church from the Jewish community into the Gentile world. The first scenes are set in Jerusalem, the last find Paul proclaiming the gospel in Rome, the capital of the world. These scenes set the boundary within which the author exploits the often high drama of the first efforts to present the message to pagans. The effective curse on Elymas the magician leads a proconsul to faith (Acts 13:6-12). The healing of a cripple evokes the mistaken belief among the heathen that Paul and Barnabus are gods and renders the occasion for an exhortation to turn to the living God (Acts 14:8-18). Imprisonment, and an earthquake, provide the stage for Paul's staccato message to the Philippian jailor "Believe in the Lord Jesus, and you will be saved, you and your household" (Acts 16:25-34). In all of these, the drama is heightened by the unanticipated opportunity to present the message and the consequent resourcefulness of the messengers. But as the narrative continues, more formal settings are provided, and two of these interest us here because they represent studied efforts at exemplary addresses, and become in fact the original models for two basic modes of presenting the gospel to pagans, the Exhortation and the Defense.

Appropriately, the Exhortation is the first of the two to appear—in Paul's speech on the Areopagus (Acts 17:22-31). The setting itself is not without significance. The Areopagus was the legendary seat of Athenian justice, and the guarantor of the constitution, rooted in religion, and thus a witness to the pagan belief in the sacred foundations of the life of society. Paul's message speaks directly to these beliefs: 1) the constitution of the world, and of society, springs from the God who made the former and ordained the latter (17:24-26); 2) God has given to all people presentiments of Himself (17:27-28); 3) God will bring justice to the world through "a man" whom he raised from the dead (17:29-31). Several features of this speech must further be observed. First, the belief that God has given all people some knowledge of Himself legitimizes the appeal to pagan poets (17:28), an appeal whose propaganda value is obvious. Second, the contrast between the true God and pagan idols just avoids a sneer at pagan credulity (17:25, 29-30). Third, with reference to Christ, the message contains only an allusion; the emphasis is upon the doctrine of God, the true God and the false gods, and upon Judgment. Fourth, the problem of pagan ignorance and knowledge is a major motif in the speech: the speech begins with pagan ignorance, later hints at the possibility of the innate knowledge of God, and finally contrasts past ignorance with the new knowledge conveyed by the present message.

The "Defense" model emerges somewhat later, as the Book of Acts describes the return of Paul to Jerusalem, his arrest, and the speeches he made in his defense. Among these is his defense before the pagan Roman governor, Felix (Acts 24:10-21). Several features of this speech become typical of later Christian apologies. 1) Disavowal of the charge: there is no proof of the charge brought against him (24:13), and those who incited the riots ought to make an accusation of actual wrongdoing (24:19-20). 2) Disclosure of his identity: he is a Christian, he worships the God of Israel; he believes the Bible, and he believes in the resurrection of the dead for reward and punishment. 3) Affirmation of good citizenship: he has always undertaken to live a harmless and wholesome life (24:16).

Paul had other opportunities to speak before governors, and we may briefly note his message. Summoned once more before Felix, and his Jewish wife Drusilla, he spoke to them of "justice, self-control, and future judgment" (Acts 24:25). After Festus had replaced Felix as governor, he invited Paul to speak before Agrippa whom Roman power had established as king over the Jews. Though Paul's defense here finds its climax in the proclamation of a suffering and risen Christ, it is comprised largely of the narrative of his own conversion (Acts 26:2-23). It was with a similar conversion narrative that Paul had made a defense before an angry mob of Jews (Acts 22:3-21).

The models for Exhortation and Defense are themselves based upon a Hellenistic-Jewish apologetic tradition which already finds some elaboration in the New Testament Epistles, most conspicuously in the Pauline account in Romans 1:18-32 of human perversion arising from idolatry. This apologetic tradition offered the early Christians a reservoir of themes with which to amplify the skeletal models in Acts. Many of these themes are embodied in the Book of Wisdom, and it will be useful to provide a short list of them here.

1) The world is created in Wisdom, which dwells with God as the "breath of His power" and the "image of His goodness" (the Logos, or Word in the early Christian message) (7:15-8:1).
2) Therefore mankind can learn of God from the works of nature so that he is without excuse for failing to come to a knowledge of God (13:1-9).
3) Idolatry is absurd and foolish—wholly contrary to reason (13:10-14:11).
4) Idolatry grew out of the desire to honor the dead who had been greatly admired (14:12-21).
5) The evil of idolatry may be seen in the destructive and irrational rituals prescribed (14:22-24) and in the moral corruption of the community (14:25-31).
6) There is thus a direct relationship between wisdom and

justice, between knowledge and morality, and rulers must seek the true wisdom that leads to justice (1:1-4; 6:12-25; 8:2-21).

7) Rulers must know above all that their power comes from God (6:1-3) and they will be punished for unjust judgments, and all unrighteousness (6:4-11; 1:5-16).

8) In spite of appearances God rewards the righteous and punishes the unrighteous, though indeed the righteous have as their greatest reward immortality and will ultimately stand in judgment on the unrighteous and on those who persecuted them (2:1-5:23).

9) Moreover, the recitation of Biblical history from the formation of the first man to the events of the life of Israel demonstrates God's providential care (10:1—12:27; 18:1-19:22) and natural disasters are the result of sin (16:1-29).

10) If the righteous suffer, it is because God is testing them, as gold is "tried by fire" (3:4-9).

It can be seen at a glance that these themes provide an embracing structure of ideas from Creation to the final Judgment. Many of them, moreover, made a particularly effective apologetic because they had analogies in popular pagan thought. There was widespread pagan acceptance of the idea that a creator could be inferred from the majesty and beauty of the world, or that wisdom was the foundation of justice, while the providential care of God for the world was frequently debated among the philosophers. Thus Jewish apologetics, and later the Christian message to the Gentiles undertook to speak as far as possible in the language of their respective audiences.

It was not until the latter part of the second century that the Exhortation and the Defense achieved a truly classic form. In the development of these genres, there was considerable experimentation in form and in the adaptation of themes from one genre to the other. Their basic structure was frequently masked by great differences in tone, and intellectual interests and assumptions, which grew out of the personality of the author. But whether Exhortation or Defense, both were written to proclaim a message. Paul's final words to Agrippa express a fundamental aim not only of exhortation, but of defense as well: "I would to God that not only you but also all who hear me this day might become such as I am [a Christian]—except for these chains" (Acts 26:29). We must also remember that while these forms contained a message ostensibly to the pagans, it is probable that in most cases the authors expected Christians also to read their work: the message to the heathen was also to be a message of encouragement and confirmation to the Christian.

The result was the growth of a vast literature from its beginnings in the second century down to the time of Augustine. The extent of this literature, the vitality of experimentation in the development of its forms, and the distinguished achievement both in artistic expression and theological reflection of its best examples, call for a lengthy treatment in this study. Hence three chapters are devoted to the "Message to the Pagans." In this chapter, we consider first the message and its presentation in two early and fairly classic examples of Defense and Exhortation. In the next chapter we shall study several variations on the forms. A third chapter will look finally at the message to the pagans in what are perhaps its two finest literary embodiments.

II

The first distinguished defense of Christianity is the "address and petition" of Justin Martyr to the Emperor Antoninus, his sons Marcus and Lucius, and the Roman Senate. As both an address and a *petitio*, Justin's *Apology* undertakes not only to defend the Christians from charges brought against them, but even more to explain who they are and what they believe—that is, to identify them— in order to free them from the iniquitous trials in which they are condemned, not for specific criminal acts, but for calling themselves Christians—for a name. But this self-identification was inevitably an opportunity for the proclamation of the message.

One of the striking features of Justin's *Apology* is the effort made to present the case for Christianity within the terms and assumptions held by his pagan readers. By the second century two schools of philosophical thought, Stoicism and Platonism, enjoyed a relatively broad popular appeal and their tenets had become somewhat intermingled. As a result, several assumptions about the nature of the world and the life of man had a considerable vogue. In particular it was widely held that the world was a rational order, even pervaded by divine rational force; that man's goal was to achieve the status of divinity, and that an essential means thereto was his personal identification with the forces of reason. It was also believed that there were spiritual intermediaries the *demons*, some of which—the good—appealed to man's intellectual and spiritual nature and so helped him in his ascent to God, while others—the evil—appealed to his physical and passionate nature and pulled him down to earth. To translate his message into these commonly understood terms of his pagan hearers, Justin placed the concept of reason at the center of his defense and organized his case around it.

He sets his perspective in the introduction where he addresses the Imperial family as "philosophers" and lovers of learning, evoking the image of Plato's "philosopher king," and reminds them of the responsibilities of true wisdom.

> 1.1[1] To the Emperor Titus Aelius Adrianus Antoninus Pius Augustus Caesar, and to his son Verissimus the philosopher, and to Lucius the philosopher, natural son of Caesar, son by adoption of Pius and a lover of learning, to the sacred Senate also and to the entire Roman people, on behalf of those from every race who are unjustly hated and shamefully treated, I, Justin, son of Priscus who was the son of Bacchius, both from Flavia Neapolis in Syria of Palestine, myself being one of them [the Christians] have prepared this address and petition.

[1]Text: PG 6.328.

Reason dictates that those who are truly pious and truly philosophers honor and love only the truth, and that they follow those who turn aside from traditional beliefs whenever they are wrong. Not only does sound reason demand that the lover of truth should not follow those who act unjustly or teach erroneous doctrines, but that he must choose, by all means, in the very face of death, even if it costs him his life, to say and do what is right. You then, take care to listen, since you are called pious and philosophers and guardians of justice and lovers of learning.

Justin complains that these philosophical rulers have failed to apply justice in the case of Christians. To explain why is to take the reader to the heart of his case: the struggle between the forces of the wicked *demons* and true reason. For Justin this is the battle between the Divine and the Satanic.

The demonic is to be seen in several aspects of heathen life and first in the mistrial of Christians. Since God is Reason and therefore preeminently rational, His enemies, the *demons* are opposed to all that is rational, and seek to disrupt orderly, rational processes. Hence in the trials of Christians as indeed in the trials of all lovers of truth, one sees only prejudice, irrationality, misjudgment:

> 1.5[2]... For us who take vows to do no harm and to hold no godless opinions, you do not hold an investigation, but, driven by an irrational passion at the instigation of evil demons, you punish us without a trial, without any consideration. Now I shall tell you the truth. Long ago evil demons appeared committing adultery with women, corrupting boys and displaying such frightening portents that those who did not judge their actions with reason were panic-stricken. Seized by fear, they did not recognize that they were evil demons, but called them gods and addressed each by whatever name the demons

[2]Text: PG 6.336.

had bestowed upon themselves. When Socrates had endeavored to expose these things by true reason and careful investigation and to turn men away from the demons, these very demons worked through men who delight in evil to have him put to death as a godless and impious man on the grounds that he was introducing new divinities. The demons work against us in a similar way. For it is not only among the Greeks in the person of Socrates that these have been confuted by reason. Among the barbarians, too, through the very same reason—which has assumed a human form in the man called Jesus Christ whom we believe—we say that the demons who have done these things are not upright, but evil and unholy; their behavior is in no way comparable to that of people who seek virtue.

If the *demons* bring about the mistrial of Christians, it is they who also stir up the persecution against those who love and live by reason:

> 57.[3] This alone can the demons do to us—make those who live without reason, who have been brought up to indulge their passions in undisciplined living, who love glory, to hate and destroy us.

The persecution and unjust trials of Christians are the immediate results of a mind hostile to reason. Since the struggle between the divine and the demonic is ultimately a battle for the mind, the *demons* have undertaken a sustained effort to achieve total control over it. Thus Justin fears they will prevent the pagans from understanding his message:

> 14[4] For we warn you to be on your guard lest the demons whom we have accused should deceive you and prevent you from coming upon these words at all or from understanding them, for they struggle to keep you as their slaves and servants, and sometimes through apparitions in dreams, sometimes through magical spells, they keep

[3] Text: PG 6.413C.
[4] Text: PG 6.348A.

in their power all those who in no way struggle for their own salvation.

In a larger view of the problem, Justin sees that the whole fabric of heathen mythology so central to the pagan mind, has been a cunning trap set by the demons who devised the tales of the gods in imitation of Christian truth—the better to deceive mankind:

> 54[5] But those who have taught the mythology created by the poets offer no proof to their students, but we demonstrate that these stories have been told under the influence of the evil demons for the deception and enslavement of the human race. For when the demons heard the prophets proclaim that Christ would come and that the ungodly would be punished by fire, they put forward the idea that many sons were born to Zeus believing that they could induce people to regard the stories about Christ as legends, just like the tales of the poets. These tales became common both among the Greeks and among all other peoples, wherever they heard the prophets foretelling faith in Christ.

There can, of course, be no divorce between the way one thinks and the way one acts—the trial of Christians alone is sufficient proof of this. But Justin goes much further to demonstrate that the immoral behavior of pagans is a direct result of their distorted thinking. We have already seen how he identified "those who live without reason" with those who "have been brought up to indulge their passions in undisciplined living." Pagans are what Christians once were: people who delighted in fornication, practiced magic, valued wealth and possessions above all things, hated and killed one another and refused to live with others of different customs. Pagan life is thus in everyway contrary to reason. To show that their way of life contradicts the basic tenet to which they subscribe—that the rational life is the good life—is to show the necessity for the alternative Christianity provides.

[5]Text: PG 6.408C.

For Christians are people who in both belief and practice are eminently reasonable. The disclosure of Christian identity is central to Justin's work as a "Defense," but the portrait of the Christians is suffused with the light of reason. At the base of Christian experience stands the Logos, the Word, in sharp contrast to the *demons*. The Word is the creative Reason at the heart of the Universe; the same Word is the Spirit that breathed in the prophets enabling them to predict future events; and that Word is also incarnated in Jesus of Nazareth who becomes therefore the authoritative Teacher of the Christians. Justin's scheme appears in summary form when he explains the origin of the Christian name:

> 12[6]...That you will be unable to divert us from our purpose, the Word makes clear, who, after the God who begot him, is the most kingly, the most just ruler we know. For just as everyone avoids poverty, suffering and disgrace, so the reasonable person refuses to do whatever the Word says should not be done. Our Teacher, I say, foretold that all these things would happen. He taught also our fathers, and is the Son and Apostle of the Lord God, Jesus Christ, from whom we Christians have received our name. We are confident of everything he has taught, since in fact many events are occurring which he had earlier predicted. This is the work of God, to predict an event which can later be shown to have happened as predicted.

We may briefly pause to note that here, as elsewhere, prophecy was to play a large part in Justin's *Apology*. Indeed Justin presents all the traditional themes of the kerygma— God and his Son, the Virgin birth, the life, death and resurrection of Christ—by a lengthy synthesis (chapters 31-52) of prophecy and fulfillment. This emphasis on prophecy should not surprise us. It was a belief widely cultivated by the Stoics that the accurate prediction of events was convincing evidence of the Divine controlling reason in

[6]Text: PG 6.344B.

the universe. Justin has appropriately adapted to his message a belief commonly held by his audience.

For Justin, Christ is preeminently the Teacher who enables his disciples to live rationally. Taught by Christ, they become chaste (chapter 15), gentle, patient and free from anger (chapter 16), and obedient to civil authorities (chapter 17). By presenting this list of virtues Justin not only denies the rumored charges that Christians are incestuous, passionate and turbulent people, but also demonstrates that Christians have the character of the ideal "rational" person, whose life was to be, in the Stoic view, unmoved by passion.

Nowhere is the Christian character more succinctly defined than in a passage to which we have already alluded:

> 14[7]. . . After putting our faith in the Word we rejected the demons, and it is now the only and unbegotten God whom we follow through his Son. Formerly we indulged in fornication, now we espouse self-control. We too employed magic; now we have entrusted ourselves to God, the unbegotten and good. We who loved the resources of money and possessions more than anything else now put our wealth into a common treasury and share with everyone in need. We who hated and killed one another and would not live with people of foreign race and customs, now, after the manifestation of Christ, make them our table companions, while we pray for our enemies, and try to lead to faith those who hate us so that they too might live according to the good precepts of Christ and with us enjoy the hope of reward which comes to all who find God, the Lord of all.

Christian life stands in sharp contrast to pagan life because it is lived in conformity with good precepts, and it does so because its controlling source is the rational Word.

Justin also identifies the Christians in terms of their rites and practices. Here, too, one sees how he attempts to meet intellectually his pagan audience by describing Christians as

---

[7]Text: PG 6.348B.

people of "enlightenment." Thus baptism is portrayed for the pagan not only as the washing away of sins, but as "enlightenment."

> 1.61[8]... This is the rationale we have learned from the apostles for baptism. Our first birth took place without our knowledge, therefore according to necessity, from the moist matrix of parental intercourse, and we were brought up among bad customs and wicked ways. So that we might not remain the children of ignorance and necessity but become children of understanding and free choice, receiving, in the water, forgiveness for the sins we have committed, the name of God, Lord and Father of all, is spoken over whoever has chosen to be born again and repented. This one name alone he speaks who leads the baptizand to the bath. For no one is able to give a name to the unnameable God. Anyone who thinks he can is a raving maniac. This bath is called "enlightenment" since those who learn these things are enlightened in their understanding. And he who is enlightened is washed also in the name of Jesus Christ crucified under Pontius Pilate, and in the name of the Holy Spirit who predicted all the things that would happen to Christ.

It is perhaps significant that Justin stresses Sunday as the day of the Christian meetings because

> 1.67[9]... it is the first day on which God, scattering the darkness and forming matter, created the world, and Jesus Christ our Savior rose from the dead on the same day. For they crucified him on the day before Saturday, while on the day after Saturday, that is on Sunday, he appeared to his apostles and disciples and taught these things which we have offered to you for your consideration

Sunday appears to be in Justin's view the day of enlightenment.

[8]Text: PG 6.421.
[9]Text: PG 6.432.

Two themes of considerable importance in the *Apology* must still be noticed. In both, the idea of Reason remains central. First, Justin speaks to his pagan audience of the resurrection and the Judgment, appealing once more to the logic of prediction and fulfillment:

> 1.52[10] Since we have now shown that all the things which have happened were predicted by the prophets, we must also believe that what has been similarly predicted as still to happen will by all means take place. Just as events have come to pass as predicted even though they were unknown, so the rest, even though they are unknown and disbelieved, will come to pass. For the prophets proclaimed two advents of Christ: in the first he would come as a man suffering and despised; but in the second when, as has been foretold, he will come from heaven with glory and with his mighty angelic host, when the dead shall rise, those who are worthy shall put on immortality, but the unrighteous he shall send to the eternal fire, to everlasting suffering, along with the evil demons.

In the second place, Justin draws on a theme whose original domicile is the Exhortation. If it is in Christian faith and practice that the divine reason is to be primarily seen, it has not been without its witness in either Jewish or pagan life. Not all who were born before Christ were without the divine reason:

> 1.46[11] . . . We have been taught that Christ is the first-born of God and I have indicated before that he is the Reason in which all people share. Those who have lived with Reason are Christians, even though they were regarded as atheists; among the Greeks, for example, Socrates and Heraclitus, and others like them, but among the barbarians, Abraham, Ananias, Azarias, Misael, Elijah, and many others whose names and deeds I pass over now since it would take too long to recount them.

[10] Text: PG 6.404D.
[11] Text: PG 6.397B.

> Conversely, those who lived long ago, but without Reason, were evil and enemies of Christ and killed those who lived with Reason.

In general, pagan life is irrational, the evidence for which is its passionate licentiousness as well as its assent to falsehoods. Justin's message is a promise of deliverance from this skein of deceptions. But Justin also believed that Reason created the world as well as all the people in it and imparted to them its own Reason. It was thus essential to Justin's message to allow for the possibility of people who lived rationally outside the faith, and to acknowledge the fact was a diplomatic overture to his audience.

To recall a theme from the Exhortation model may serve to remind us that Justin's *Apology* as a whole belongs rather to the defense genre. If we have lost sight of the fact, it is perhaps because Justin has made his defense serve what appears a much more pressing goal, that of presenting the message of Christian faith to his readers in the imagery and themes familiar to them of the philosopher's quest for the rational way of life. On reflection, however, we can see how deftly the argument has included the proper elements. Justin's attack on pagan irrationality is a somewhat ironic disavowal of the charge: that the charge is false follows from the perverse way in which pagans attack the Christians. In a more direct way, Justin disavows the charge by describing the Christian way of life. The disclosure of Christian identity entails an affirmation of good citizenship and a wholesome way of life. It also provides the motivation for the outline of the kerygma, with special emphasis upon the doctrine of the Judgment. We can recognize here, then, a fresh development, but the essential content, of Paul's speech before Felix. The idea of reason has been merely the thematic focus for an already historic message.

III

We turn now to Clement of Alexandria (ca 150-215 AD) to observe in his *Protrepticus* (*Exhortation to the Greeks*), what is perhaps the purest example of the Exhortation in Patristic literature, a work which forces into a classical mold the themes adumbrated by St. Paul. The work is also of special interest to us because it illustrates a sharp consciousness of the close relation between medium and message.

The Exhortation as a form by which one leads an audience to a decision is not without classical precedents. Scholars have argued that Aristotle's lost *Protrepticus* might well have provided an example for Clement, and other Greeks as well are known to have written Exhortations—Epicurus, and such leaders of Stoic thought as Cleanthes, Chrysippus and Posidonius. However, the dominating themes of Clement's *Exhortation* are not classical but Christian and find their fundamental parallels in the speech of St. Paul on the Areopagus. A Greek rhetorical structure is, of course, imposed on the material. We shall speak later of the Introduction—the technical rhetorical term is "*proemium*"— (chapter 1), and the Conclusion (chapter 12). The main argument is comprised of both a "confirmation" (chapters 2-9), where evidence is produced to establish the case, and a rebuttal of anticipated objections (chapters 10-11). But chapters 2-11 function as a thematic unity in which Clement attacks the pagan religions and the gods made by "the art and imagination of men," as Paul had earlier done; affirms the Christian God, demonstrating that this affirmation is anticipated by the pagan poets and philosophers; charges the pagans with ignorance, and calls upon them to repent in view of a coming Judgment.

These themes are not, of course, presented as an arid argument. Clement was writing an Exhortation and seems to have been keenly aware of the power of "atmosphere," color, and tone in effecting a decision. We shall see presently how Clement finds in music an image in which medium and message blend into one another. At the moment, while tracing the themes, we must observe one of the ways Clement invests his message with an emotional appeal growing directly out of the subject matter: he stimulates in the reader a sense of movement from the heart of darkness into a glorious light.

If we turn first to the Rebuttal we can see at once the axis on which this movement is made to rest. It is quite simply that pagan religion entails ignorance and immorality, Christian faith knowledge and godliness:

> X[12] Let us not, then, let us not be reduced to abject slavery nor become swinish, but as true born children of the light let us gaze upward and look at the light lest the Lord prove us bastards as the sun the eagles. Let us regain our senses and move from ignorance to knowledge, from folly to wisdom, from indulgence to self-control, from unrighteousness to righteousness, from godlessness to God.

In the Confirmation Clement organizes his material upon a distinction familiar through classical precedent: he discusses the gods of the people, the gods of the philosophers, and the gods of the poets. These he places in contrast to the true God of the prophets. The order of the discussion thus determined facilitated the gradual movement from a sense of darkness to one of light.

Clement begins his attack on pagan religion by an exposé of the mystery religions. He deepens the sense of darkness here by protesting against their secrecy: the veil commonly drawn over them is a symbol of the darkness in which they shroud the spiritual life of pagans. It is the act of a Christian to bring the mysteries out of the shadows:

> 11.[13] What if I should recount the mysteries for you? I shall not betray them in mockery, as they say Alcibiades did, but I shall strip quite bare, as the truth warrants, the quackery concealed in them and shall bring out on the stage of life for spectators to see those you call your gods, to whom the mystic rites belong.

Clement goes on to mock the absurdities of the gods of the common people as they have been "created" by philosophers, poets and artists, and to expose them for what they

[12]Text: LCL, ed. Butterworth, p. 202.
[13]Text: LCL, 28.

are—on the one hand, dead men whom long time has led to popular veneration, and on the other, materials of earth carved into human shape by artists. The attack on art ("when art flourished, error increased" (chapter 4) has its roots much more in Biblical than in Platonist thought, passages, for example, in the Old Testament and Book of Wisdom which mock the "senseless" idols, and derives its authority, at this point in the message, from the Pauline model in Acts.

> IV.[14] The image-makers dishonor the senseless earth, pervert it from its proper nature and through their craft induce men to worship it. For in my view, those who make gods do not worship gods and divinities, but earth and art, which is what statues are. For a statue truly is lifeless matter given shape by a craftsman's hand. For us, however, there are no statues appealing to the senses made from matter perceived by the senses, but One who is perceived by the mind. For God—the only true God—is perceived by the mind not the senses.

But we observe a major shift in tone as Clement discusses the gods of the philosophers. These too, it is true, have betrayed their ignorance by making gods out of the principles on which the universe is constructed whether those are the material elements, or abstract principles such as the Infinite, "Fulness and Vacuity," or the "Soul" of the Universe.

> VI.[15] But a vast crowd of this sort comes rushing towards me like some monster in a dream, bringing an apparition of strange divinities, and chattering the nonsensical fantasies of an old woman.

Yet the philosophers have expressed sentiments which, borrowed from the Hebrews, show that God is "not far from them."

[14]Text: LCL, 116.
[15]Text: LCL. 150.

VI[16] I seek God, not the works of God. Whom, then, of your men am I to take as a helper in my search?—for I have not completely despaired of you Plato, perhaps. . . . And now, philosophy, hasten to provide not this one Plato alone, but many others who cry out by divine inspiration—since they have somehow laid hold of the truth—that God is in truth one and only.

Poetry, too, though it is "completely occupied with falsehood," (chapter 7) still speaks of God. Clement expresses the ambiguity thus:

VII[17] For if the Greeks have received generally some sparks of the divine Reason and thus have voiced bits of the truth, they bear witness to the fact that the power of the truth has not lain hidden away, at the same time they convict themselves of their own weakness in that they have not arrived at its end.

Throughout chapter 7 Clement gives numerous quotations from the poets which demonstrate the Christian God and, in doing so, he echoes the appeal of Paul to the poets in his message on the Areopagus to the Athenians. At the same time he evokes the dark-light theme by the striking word *enausma*, sparks, used of lighting a fire.

Gradually, then, we have been emerging from the deepest darkness of the pagan mysteries into the obscured light of the pagan conscience witnessed in its philosophy and poetry. We are ready now to step into the pure light of prophetic truth. Even here the gradation continues, for Clement begins by quoting a prophecy from the famed Sibyl, regarded by the Christians as a divinely inspired Gentile source of truth. He concludes this "ascent into the light" with the voices of the canonical prophets. It is the words of Scripture, simple and unadorned, which have saving power:

[16]Text: LCL. 152, 158.
[17]Text: LCL. 166.

VIII.[18] Now that we have duly completed our review of other literature, it is time to come to the prophetic writings. The divine oracles provide for us the starting point of piety and lay the foundations of the truth. For the divine writings and the mode of life they recommend are short-cuts to salvation. Stripped of all stylistic adornment, without either suave fluency or seductive flattery, they nevertheless raise up a man bound down by evil. They look down upon the slippery paths of life and with one and the same voice heal many sicknesses, turning us away from deception which harms, clearly exhorting us to the salvation set before us.

It is here, through the prophetic voices, that the true God is at last set forth as "the God who made the world and everything in it, being Lord of heaven and earth," who "does not live in shrines made by man" but gives to all life and breath, and is "not far from each one of us" for "in Him we live and move and have our being" and "we ought not to think that the Deity is like gold, or silver, or stone" (Acts 17:24-29). Clement chooses the prophetic Scriptures to echo the Pauline message:

VIII.[19] Jeremiah the all-wise prophet, or rather the Holy Spirit in Jeremiah, points to God: " 'I am a God near at hand,' he says 'and not a God far off. . . Do I not fill the heavens and the earth' says the Lord" [Jer 23:23]. . . What does the Holy Spirit say through Hosea [Amos]? I shall not hesitate to say: "Behold I am the one who strengthens the thunder and creates the wind" whose hands have established the host of heaven [Amos 4:13]. . . Through Isaiah he says: "I am God and there is no other" [Isa 45:22]. . . He is vexed with idolaters and says: "To whom have you likened the Lord and to what likeness have you likened him? Has not the carpenter made the image, the goldsmith melted the gold and gilded it? [Isa 40:18-19].

[18]Text: LCL. 172.
[19]Text: LCL. 174.

This exposition of truth demands decision, and as Paul concluded his message to the Athenians with a call to repentance in the face of judgment, so Clement asks for decisions in view of the awful Day approaching:

> IX[20] Since Moses confesses that it was with fear and trembling that he heard *about* the Word, do you not fear when you actually listen *to* the Word? Are you not concerned? Do you not take care, do you not hasten to learn, to hasten, that is, to salvation? Do you not fear wrath; do you not love grace; do you not covet hope, so that you might escape the Judgment?... What else remains for unbelievers but condemnation and judgment?

We must note finally, that within the exposition of chapters 2-9, it is only now that the figure of Christ emerges with clarity as Savior in the face of judgment. Even the words of the prophets lack lustre beside the brilliant light of *His* proclamation of the Day of the Lord:

> IX[21] No one would be so impressed by the exhortations of the other holy men as by the Lord himself, the lover of mankind. For he has no other concern than our salvation. He himself urges us to salvation, crying out, "The kingdom of heaven is at hand!" [Mt 4:17]. He converts those who in fear draw near to him.

It is clear that within these chapters of Confirmation Clement delivers to the pagans a message highly studied in both its manner and themes. The progression in the atmosphere from darkness to light is intended to provide an emotional context alive with movement and energy and hence conducive to persuasion. In its major themes, Clement's message has the powerful simplicity of Paul's message to the Athenians. It is a message about one God in the face of idolatry, a God who is creator of the world and has implanted in man an intimation of Himself. It is a message about repentance and judgment, and about a Savior who can rescue mankind from impending destruction. As in

[20] Text: LCL. 182.
[21] Text: LCL. 192.

Paul's speech, so here in Clement's *Exhortation*, Christology is ultimately crucial to the message, but it plays a secondary role in its presentation.

Clement has enriched the simplicity of these themes by casting them under the light of presuppositions which, to some extent, were shared by his pagan contemporaries. Two of these, reflected in chapter 1, make their presence felt at various points throughout the *Exhortation*.

First, there had been a long tradition within Hellenistic thought which stressed the community between the gods and men, and saw, especially in the development of the potential of the human mind, the possibility of a sort of divinization of man. Clement has adapted the view to the Christian *mythos*. Because man is made in the image of God, his destiny, when fulfilled, is to enjoy the life of God and thus become like God. But idolatry has deflected man's vision from God to the things of earth. The loss of the vision of God has separated man from God, and deprived him therefore of the life of God. The result is death and destruction. For Clement, the impending destruction is as much one's own eternal death, already reflected in the despicable quality of life seen in idolatry, as it is the future eschatological judgment. The message of the gospel is thus a message of salvation from all forces that destroy and corrupt our lives, a message which restores our vision of God and sets us once more on the path to a life which is full because it is lived with God.

> 1.[22] This is the new Song, the epiphany of the Word which was in the beginning and before the beginning, an epiphany which now has cast its light among us. For the Savior who was before has appeared just now, the One who is in "Him who is" (for "the Word was with God" [Jn 1:1]) has appeared as our Teacher, the Word by whom all things were created has appeared, our Creator who in the beginning not only formed us but gave us life. His epiphany as Teacher has illuminated for us the path to

---

[22] Text: LCL. 16.

"living well," so that as God he might later lead us to everlasting life. Not that now for the first he has pitied us for our error. From the very beginning he pitied us, but now through his epiphany he has saved those who are perishing. For right to the present time, that wicked beast, the serpent, beguiles, enslaves and outrageously abuses mankind, bringing upon him a thoroughly barbarous punishment, like those who are said to bind dead bodies to their prisoners of war until they rot together with the bodies. Those he can get in his power from their very birth, this wicked and tyrannical snake binds to sticks and stones and images and idols of every kind, binding them tightly with the terrible chains of fear of demons; then, as it is said, he brings them to the grave and buries them alive with their idols until they disintegrate together.

Second, Greek philosophy could produce many variations on the common theme that the world must be understood as a balanced and harmonious whole. One sees, for example, an expression of the theme in psychological and political terms in a work such as Plato's *Republic*, or in physical terms in the Stoic view of a universe perfectly ordered by reason. Consequently, for Clement the message of salvation is a call for the restoration of the world and of mankind to perfect proportion and balance of the parts. At the center of this restoration is the Word of God, the melodious speech which created the world as a harmonious whole and by whom man can become the divine instrument he was made to be:

> 1.[23] See how powerful the new song is. It has made men from stones, men from wild beasts. Those who were, in reality, dead, who had no share in what is truly life, came to life if only they heard the Word. This has arranged all things harmoniously, and brought into tune the dissonant elements, so that the whole world might be in harmony with it... The Word of God, who was from David

[23]Text: LCL. 10.

> yet before him, despised the lyre and the cithara, instruments without life, but rather tuned this world and its counterpart man, soul and body, in harmony with the Holy Spirit. He now praises God through a richly melodious instrument and sings in harmony with his instrument, man...The Lord made man a living instrument after his own likeness, for the Word is himself an instrument of God, of perfect harmony, melodious and pure, a heavenly wisdom beyond this world.

In Clement, as in Justin, we have an instructive example of an attitude apparently common in the second century: the message to the pagans must declare the historic faith of the Church, but the messenger must also endeavor to build bridges to his audience with at least some images available to the experience of both. We have no statistics to demonstrate how far this approach actually effected conversions, but that it enriched the message, there can be no doubt.

We must turn finally to a feature of the Exhortation which suggests some very careful reflection on an ambiguity inherent in the presentation of the message, specifically in the relation between the words in which the message is conveyed, and "The Word" it is intended to convey.

We catch a hint of the ambiguity already in the Introduction (chapter 1). Here Clement defines his "Song" in contrast to the songs of such fabled minstrels of antiquity as Arion and Orpheus. If their songs had strange powers to allure the fishes (Arion) and charm the beasts (Orpheus) the "New Song" has power to change those who have degenerated into beasts back into true humans. In this context the New Song is defined clearly as the Word of God: "What then does this instrument, which is the Word of God, the Lord, and the New Song, desire?" (*Exhortation* 1 [LCL]). But within a few lines an ambiguity arises, as Clement insists that, if he calls his Song "new," it has an antiquity greater than that of the singers of Greek legend: "But do not suppose that my Song of Salvation is new in the way a house or a vase is new. For the Word was 'in the beginning, and "before the morning star," it was with God and was God'[Jn

1:1]. But error is old while the truth appears new." Here the possessive "my" suggests a double sense for the word "Song"—both the Divine Word, as he immediately explains, but also, if less obviously, Clement's own *Exhortation*.

In the Conclusion (chapter 12) this ambiguity appears as a creative tension between the Divine Word and *His* Song on the one hand, and the human messenger on the other. Clement brings his Exhortation to a close with a highly rhetorical appeal. He contrasts in a vivid extended image the madness of the Dionysiac revels with the glorious worship of the saints gathered about the Word. At first, it is Clement himself who issues the call to repentance, promising to reveal, in place of the mysteries of Dionysus the Word Himself:

> XII[24] I would pity him [Pentheus, King of Thebes, compelled by Dionysus to become his devotee] drunk with wine and quite demented and I would call him back to salvation and to his senses, for the Lord welcomes the repentance of a sinner and not his death. Come, madman, no more the thyrsus, no more the ivy wreath; cast away the mitre, cast away the fawnskin [accoutrements of the revelers], return to your senses! I shall show you the Word and the mysteries of the Word, comparing them with your own mysteries.

The last words are important: the object of the messenger, as of his message is to reveal Christ, the Truth. In the best circumstances, the message moves beyond merely pointing to the Truth until it so embodies the truth that it becomes Christ himself speaking. The tension between the medium and the object it conveys is dissolved in a creative union of the two. This ideal motivates, I believe, the progress of the rhetoric in the following passage, where out of the vision offered by the messenger (Clement) the living Word himself appears and speaks. Turning to Pentheus' companion, Tiresias, the old blind seer, Clement cries:

[24]Text: LCL. 254.

XII[25] You too, old man, come to me! Cast away your prophetic art, your Dionysiac frenzy. Leave Thebes. Be guided to the truth. Look! I give you the cross as the staff to lean upon. Hurry, Tiresias, believe! You will receive your sight. Christ shines more brightly than the sun; through him the eyes of the blind are opened. Night will flee from you, fire will fear you, and death depart. You, reverend sir, who do not see Thebes will see the heavens.

Oh! True mysteries and holy! Unclouded light! I am given the light to see the mystic vision of the realms above and of God; I am sanctified in the sacred rites of initiation, but the Lord instructs and seals the mystic, lighting his way, and entrusts the believer to the Father's eternal care. These are the revels of my mysteries.

If you wish, you, too, may be initiated, and you will dance with the angels about the unbegotten and incorruptible and only true God, while the Word of God will sing along with us. This everlasting Jesus, the one great high priest of the one God and Father, prays for mankind and exhorts them: "Hear, you multitudes of peoples, or rather all rational men and women, both Greeks and barbarians. I call every race of man whom I have created by the will of the Father. Come to me, and find your true place under the one God and the one Word of God. Then you will no longer rank above the beasts only in the possession of reason, for I give to you alone of all living creatures the fruit of immortality to enjoy. I wish, I long to share with you this gift, too, providing you with the full benefit of incorruptibilty. I give you reason; I give you myself, the perfect knowledge of God. This I am, this God desires, this is concord, this the harmony of the Father, this the Son, this the Word of God, the arm of the Lord, the power of all things, the will of the Father. Of this you long ago were images, though not in every way corresponding. I wish to restore you again to the original form so that you may be like me. I shall anoint you with the oil of faith by which you cast off corruption, and I shall show

[25]Text: LCL. 256.

you the pure form of righteousness through which you ascend to God. 'Come to me all you that labor and are heavily burdened and I will give you rest. Take my yoke upon yourselves and learn from me, because I am meek and humble of heart and you will find rest for your souls. For my yoke is easy and my burden is light'"[Mt 11:28-30].

For Clement, then, the message is conveyed by a medium (language and form) whose highest goal is to present the Christ in the immediate power of His own compelling light. If in this glorious vision we lose sight of the medium, it is not because the medium itself is unimportant. On the contrary, as the passage above reveals, Clement uses all the artifice of rhetoric at his command, for it is through form and language that the light of Christ shines forth. Indeed, the entire *Exhortation* is replete with images and rhetorical ornamentation, and at points becomes virtually a prose poem. For Clement the medium both imitates and embodies the music of the New Song.

Suggestions for Further Reading

Daniélou, J., *Gospel Message and Hellenistic Culture.* Trans. J.A. Baker. London and Philadelphia 1973.

Daniélou shows how apologetic literature endeavored to formulate a missionary message. Special attention is given to Justin and Clement. There is a full bibliography.

Goodenough, E.R., *The Theology of Justin Martyr.* Jeno 1923.

Chapter 3 describes the contribution made by Hellenistic Judaism to Justin's message to the pagans.

Ferguson, John, *Clement of Alexandria.* TWAYNE, New York 1974.

An outline of the life and writings of Clement.

Osborne, E.F., *The Philosophy of Clement of Alexandria.* Cambridge 1957.

Chapters 10-13 are a good discussion on the relationships among Faith, Knowledge and Truth in Clement's thought.

Lilla, Salvatore R.C., *Clement of Alexandria. A Study in Christian Platonism and Gnosticism*, Oxford 1971.

A first-rate study of Clement's thought. Chapter 1 shows the background to Clement's positive evaluation of Greek Philosophy.

Chapter Four

THE MESSAGE TO THE PAGANS II

As Christianity gained numerical strength, it increasingly attracted the attention of pagans. From a modern Christian point of view, pagans rather generally misconceived the nature of early Christianity. At one level, many were content to accept rumors which identified Christians as incestuous, brutal and atheistic—the excerpt above from Apuleius reflects what must have been a common conception. As time passed, however, some cultured pagans felt compelled to take a sufficiently serious view of Christianity to enter into dialogue and debate with Christians. There is no reason to doubt the historical reality of Justin's debate with Crescens to which he alludes in his second *Apology*. A little later (ca. 180 A.D.) the pagan Celsus published a book, the *True Discourse*, as an attack upon Christianity. In a Christian work written about the same time, Theophilus, according to Eusebius the seventh bishop of Antioch, describes a dialogue with a cultivated pagan, Autolycus. The *Octavius* of Minucius Felix, from the first half of the third century, represents a pagan in debate with a Christian, and seems to regard the dialogue-debate as a normative way to present the message to pagans. Thus during the second century, pagans had begun to address the problems they perceived in Christian faith and practice.

There was, for example, the problem of culture and education. This problem, as seen by the pagans, had wide ramifications. Many pagans despised the Christians as simple-minded people, possibly even the dupes of quacks and jugglers, who nevertheless professed a knowledge not unlike that of the philosophers and expected educated pagans to take their message seriously. Their knowledge, however, did not appear to be rooted in the great tradition of classical literature which acquired some validation by its sheer artistic power. To the pagans Christians seemed deliberately to spurn the Greek and Roman classics. They produced an authentication for their views rather in the Bible which the pagans regarded as the barbaric writings of an insignificant people. Some of their views, indeed, could find no support in methods of reasoning established in pagan schools. The pagans mocked at nothing more persistently than the Christian doctrine of the Last Judgment and the Resurrection of the Dead, the latter of which in particular was outside all the bounds of normal reasoning. The problem of culture thus led back ultimately to epistemology.

Pagans also complained that Christian faith was disruptive to the social order. The complaint took various forms: that the Christians were an actively hostile element in the state, a faction serving a "king" other than Caesar, or that the Christians were uncooperative in the social life of the community, and unproductive in the economic life of the state. Increasingly, the pagans feared that Christians were alienating the gods, and bringing upon the state disasters sent in anger by the divine powers—defeat in battle, famine, flood, disease.

In the many variations on the primitive forms of the message to the pagans, we can see the efforts Christians made to respond to concerns such as these. Of course, in all the variations, one recognizes the fundamental pattern of the Christian message with emphasis upon God the Creator and God the Judge while the figure of Christ appears in different degrees of importance, and is sometimes, indeed, entirely omitted. But the pagan challenge forced other themes also to acquire importance in the message. In this

chapter we shall consider several authors whose work, vary-
ing widely in artistic quality as in theological depth, reflects
the Christian effort to speak to pagan concerns. The selections offered will emphasize especially the place in the message of such themes as: the nature of Christian knowledge,
reason and revelation; the truth, authority, and dignity of
the Bible as the intellectual foundation of the Christian way
of life, and the corresponding failure of classical culture; the
reliability of the Christian eschatological hopes; the Christian way of life as a constructive force in society, in contrast
to the corruption of pagan life; the interpretation of events
to establish a true theodicy. In the discussion of these
themes we shall find at points that the Fathers continued to
show a lively interest in the problems of presenting the
message, and of this, too, we must take note.

Tatian and Theophilus

Tatian's *Discourse to the Greeks* (ca. 170 A.D.) is one of
the most vitriolic messages to be addressed to pagans.
Tatian's anger apparently grows out of the sting he has felt
from the pagan ridicule of his lack of intellectual and cultural sophistication. Accordingly, he turns the tables on the
pagans and shows that all their sophistication has not
brought them to the truth as their contentions show:

> 26.[1] Stop parading the words of others and adorning
> yourselves like the jackdaw with feathers not your own. If
> each city takes from you its own contribution to your
> speech, you will be unable to carry on your captious
> arguments. You ask who God is, and do not know even
> what is within you. You gape into the heavens, and
> stumble into pits. Your libraries are like labyrinths, but
> the readers of your books like sieves...
>
> Why are my words objectionable, when you are quite
> ready to dismiss everything else? Are you not born like us,

[1]Text: TU IV.27.

and share in the same administration of the world? Why
do you say that wisdom is with you alone when you enjoy
the same sun, the same stars as others, and neither is your
birth more distinguished than, nor your death preferable
to, that of other men. Your nonsense originates with your
elementary school teachers, and while you divide out
your own wisdom you have been separated from the true
wisdom. Your schools of wisdom are named after men.
You do not know God, but destroy one another fighting
among yourselves. Therefore you are nothing at all. You
steal each other's words, and argue like the blind man
with the deaf...

When we recognized that you were people of this kind,
we left you. We are no longer interested in your literature,
but we follow the Word of God.

Here it is only in the final words that Tatian becomes at all
helpful in presenting a Christian alternative. But he goes on
to explain the grounds of his belief in a short account of his
conversion. In contrast to all the pretensions of Greek learning and culture, the simple word of the Bible alone had for
him the ring of truth. Having acknowledged his disenchant-
ment with Greek religion, he confesses:

29.[2] When I found myself alone, I wondered how I
might discover the truth. As I was searching diligently, I
happened to come upon some barbarian writings [the
Bible] older than the teachings of the Greeks, too divine
to share in their errors. And I came to believe them
because of the simplicity of the language and the artlessness of the writers, the sensible account of creation, the
prediction of future events, the extraordinary character
of the precepts, and their witness to the administration of
all things by one God. Since my soul was taught of God, I
understood that the literature of the Greeks leads to
condemnation, while the writings of the Christians frees
the world from enslavement.

[2]Text: TU IV.29.

It is important to note that Tatian's message is not one that calls for irrational faith. On the one hand, his message seeks its own standards for measuring the truth: simplicity and artlessness, in contrast to the intellectual dances of the Greeks. On the other, Tatian also employs grounds for belief acceptable to many pagans. As we have seen, pagans accepted prediction and fulfillment as rational evidence; and some at least would have agreed that a lofty ethic and a vision of the multitudinous parts of the universe leading back to a single ground of Being fulfilled the standards of truth.

In the three books of Theophilus *To Autolycus* we have the elaboration of a discussion with a distinguished pagan. The setting is suggestive of the kinds of circumstances in which a Christian might present the message to the pagans:

> 11.1[3] Some time ago, my good Autolycus, we had a discussion in which you wanted to learn about my God. You listened for a little while to my discourse and I set out for you my practice of religion. Then we bade one another farewell, and departed each to his own house as good friends, though you had been rather harsh towards me at first. You know and remember that you thought my talk was folly. Since you encouraged me to do so, though I have little skill in discourse, I should like to point out to you more precisely through this book the vain labor of your religion and the vain worship in which you are held. At the same time, through a few of your own history books, which perhaps you read but do not yet understand, I shall try to make the truth clear to you.

Theophilus' work is distinguished by its long historical disquisitions in Books II and III. History was used in the New Testament, for example by the martyr Stephen, to present the message to the Jews and to accent their blindness and hardness of heart. In Theophilus, the sketches of the history of man provide a rack on which to hang an exposition of a broad range of Christian doctrines. But the imme-

---

[3]Text: *Theophilus of Antioch Ad Autolycum*, ed. R. M. Grant, OECT, 22.

diate rationale for introducing this record of human history
is to establish a contrast between the profane knowledge of
the pagans and the inspired knowledge of Christians, indeed
between the classical cultural heritage as a whole and the
Biblical. Book II begins by recalling pagan stories about the
gods and the origin of the world—whether these stories
emerge from the people, from philosophers, or from
poets—while a pagan chronology shows how pagan families
derive their names from fables giving them divine descent.
Repeatedly Theophilus contrasts the two cultures. For
example:

> 11.8.[4] And what am I to say of the multitude which yet
> remains of such names and genealogies? In every way all
> their writers and poets and so-called philosophers are
> deceived, as well as those who pay any attention to them.
> They have concocted legends and fantastic tales about
> their gods, and shown them not as gods but as men, in
> some cases drunkards, in others fornicators and murder-
> ers. Concerning the origin of the world, they have said
> stupid and inconsistent things. Some have declared the
> world uncreated, as I said before. Those who say it is
> uncreated and eternal contradict those who teach that it
> was created. They have said this from conjecture and
> human calculation, and not in accordance with the
> truth...   11.9 But men of God who had received the
> Holy Spirit and become prophets, were breathed upon by
> God himself and granted wisdom. They were holy and
> just, and God was their teacher. Wherefore they were
> thought worthy to receive this reward, that they should
> be the instruments of God and a dwelling place for his
> wisdom through which they spoke both about the crea-
> tion of the world, and everything else—for they also
> predicted plagues and famines and wars. There were not
> merely one or two but many from many different periods
> among the Hebrews, while among the Greeks the Sibyl
> was such a prophet. Their words were all in agreement,

[4]Text: OECT, 34.

whether they spoke about the past, the present or the future. Accordingly we are persuaded that the future will turn out as predicted, just as the past.

Or again:

> 11.33[5] Who then of the so-called wise men and poets and historians could have spoken the truth when they lived after the events...
> 11.35. But it is possible to see how all the prophets spoke in agreement since it was through one and the same Spirit that they spoke both about the creation of the world and man and about the administration of all things by one God... Now these of whom we have spoken were prophets, uneducated and ignorant, mere keepers of sheep.

In Book III Theophilus works out a remarkable chronology (revealing that the world had in his day seen 5698 years and a few odd months and days since its creation!) to demonstrate that Christian history is based on more ancient and authoritative documents than pagan. This leads to a concluding attack on pagan intellectual culture as a whole:

> 111.30[6] But the Greeks have not mentioned the true histories, in the first place because they themselves confess that they discovered the alphabet either among the Chaldaeans, or Egyptians, or Phoenicians; and in the second place, because they blundered and still blunder in not speaking about God but about vain and useless matters. They speak with great reverence of Homer and Hesiod and the rest of the poets but the incorruptible and only God of glory they have not only forgotten but even slander. They persecuted, and still to this day, persecute those who worship him. Worse, they bestow honors and prizes on those who mock God in elegant language, while of those who strive for virtue and practice holy living, some they have stoned, some put to death, and to the

[5]Text: OECT, 82.
[6]Text: OECT, 146.

present time subject them to cruel tortures. Of necessity
such people have lost the wisdom of God and have not
found the truth.

Theophilus recognizes here that the "failure" of classical
culture stems from the blindness and perversity of the
pagans in pursuing idolatry. Indeed the last phrases of the
passage just quoted recall the similar strictures of Stephen
and Paul against the Jews. In Book I Theophilus had
already considered in some detail the problem of reason and
revelation in faith. On the one hand, he affirms (in words
echoing Paul in both Acts 17 and Romans 1) that nature
herself is a sufficient revelation of the existence of God. On
the other hand he recognizes that the sinfulness of pagans
has destroyed their sight:

> 1.2[7]. . . God is seen by those who are able to see him
> when the eyes of their soul have been opened. All indeed
> have eyes, but some have cataracts, as it were, and do not
> see the light. But just because the blind do not see does
> not mean that the sun does not shine. The blind should
> blame themselves and their eyes. So you, good sir, have
> spiritual cataracts because of your sins and wicked deeds.

> 1.5[8] Just as man's soul is not seen since it is invisible to
> us, but is inferred from the movement of the body, so also
> God cannot be seen by human eyes, but is seen and
> recognized from his foreknowledge and his deeds. When
> one has seen a boat on the sea, with sails adjusted and
> moving purposely towards the harbor, he concludes it
> has a pilot who is guiding it. So we must infer that God is
> the pilot of the whole universe, even though he is not seen
> by our bodily eyes since no space holds him. . .

> 1.6 Consider then his works, the regular rotation of the
> seasons, and the change of climate, the orderly movement
> of the stars, the passage of days and nights, months and
> years, the varied beauty of seeds, and plants and fruits,

[7]Text: OECT, 2.
[8]Text: OECT, 6.

the many kinds of creatures—those that walk, fly, crawl, swim in fresh or salt water—the instinct animals have for procreation and the nourishment of their young, and this not for their own advantage but for man's, the providence by which God has prepared food for all beings, or the wonderful plan by which all things are subject to the human race...

1.7 This God is the Lord of all, who alone has stretched out the heavens [Job 9:8] and who has established the breadth of the world below it [Job 38:18], who stirs the depths of the sea and makes its waves roar [Ps 65:7], who rules its strength and calms the surge of the waters [Ps 89:9], who has established the earth upon the waters [Ps 24:2], and given breath to nourish it—whose breathing nourishes everything. If he should restrain his breath everything would fail [Job 34:14, 15]. It is of this one you speak, his breath you breathe, yet you do not know him. This is the result of the blindness of your soul and the hardness of your heart.

Theophilus' critique of pagan culture begins with the question of knowing. Accordingly, his message calls for a radical readjustment of vision, a mental re-formation grounded in Biblical knowledge, as a result of which we can perceive the world aright.

Origen, Against Celsus

We meet again these two related problems of knowledge and culture in Origen's work *Against Celsus* (ca. 250 A.D.). The book is an attempt to answer point by point the objections to Christianity Celsus had listed in his *True Discourse* 70 years earlier. Origen wrote in the first instance to strengthen the faith of Christians against Celsus' attack, but we must consider the work here because it is a reply to Celsus and has much to say about both the nature of the message and its presentation.

From the quotations Origen gives of Celsus' work, we

gather that Celsus repeatedly scoffed at Christianity as a religion for the simpleminded, full of absurdities, and quite irrational. Just as Theophilus' pagan contemporaries associated the simpleminded Christians with the rude culture of the Hebrews, so Celsus not only attacked the simplicity of mind but also the cultural inferiority of the Judaeo-Christian tradition. In fact, he had set passages of Plato beside passages from the Scriptures to demonstrate that the Greeks had found better expressions for similar ideas. He argued that the Hebrews had borrowed from the Greeks, but in borrowing had been unable to maintain the high quality of Greek thought. The argument implied, and claimed, the superiority of Greek culture.

The heart of Origen's answer to Celsus' criticism lies in the distinction he makes between faith and knowledge, between two classes of hearers to whom the message is directed, the multitude in whom the message is intended simply to inspire faith, and those advanced in Christian knowledge who know the deep things of God. The Scriptures contain truth of more than one kind, and at the deepest level provide a vision far nobler than anything which has come from Greek culture. This vision, however, is only for the initiated. The message to the heathen must be presented at the most superficial level of understanding. The deep secrets of God are not to be revealed to the pagans. In the light of this distinction, it is not surprising that Origen also insists on Christian knowledge, and therefore Christian culture, as *sui generis*: the Christian message is not comprised of the propositions of Greek philosophy, but is a word fertilized by the inspiration of the Holy Spirit and so effective to kindle a fire in the soul and transform character. Like Theophilus, Origen insists that pagan misunderstanding of the message arises from the veil over the eyes, from their indisposition to see its simple truth. Even so, the message is not irrational, nor absurd, but can be presented through the normal intellectual processes of dialectic and discussion. The Christian literary inheritance, moreover, can establish its worth not only on the grounds of its surpassing wisdom, but on the pagan's own ground: its antiquity. Here once more, Origen strikes a theme that persists in the Christian message to the heathen. A catena of passages from Book VI will illustrate these points.

> VI.2[9] I have said this against the charge made by Celsus and others of the plain style of the Scriptures, since their splendor seems to be diminished by comparison with artful diction. For our prophets, Jesus, and his apostles, kept in view the character of the message which not only embraces the truth but has the power to win over the multitude. Once persuaded and instructed, each, according to his ability, ascends to the ineffable mysteries contained in the apparent simplicity of the language. Indeed, if I may speak boldly, the beautiful and studied diction of Plato and others like him has benefited very few—if indeed one can speak of "benefit" at all—while many have received help from the speech of those who have taught or written simply but at the same time with sure aim and effective force. Thus you will find Plato in the hands of those who regard themselves as philologians, but Epictetus is admired by anyone who comes upon him looking for help, sensing in his words the source of their own improvement. I do not say this to slander Plato, for most of the world has found him helpful, but rather to point to the intent of those who say, "My speech and my message came not in the plausible words of wisdom, but in demonstration of the Spirit and power, that your faith might not rest in the wisdom of men but in the power of God" [I Cor. 2:4,5]. For the divine Word says that the spoken word itself, however true and trustworthy it may be, cannot reach the human heart unless some power from God is given to the speaker and grace adorns the speech, a grace which apart from God cannot come to those who speak with power. For the prophet says in Psalm 67 "The Lord will give a word to those who preach the gospel with much power" [Ps 68:12]. Granted that in some respects the Greeks teach the same things as we, yet

[9]Text: SC 147.180.

their teachings have not the same power to subdue the heart and conform the life to their words. Accordingly, Jesus' disciples, though ignorant of Greek philosophy, traveled through many nations of the world and, in accordance with the Word, disposed the hearts of their hearers in the way each deserved. Their hearers became much better persons in proportion to the inclination of their own free will to receive the good.

VI.4.[10] But those "wise men" who have written such things about the Highest Good go down to the Piraeus to pray to Artemis as though to God, and to look upon festivities celebrated by ignorant people... But our most ancient wise men, Moses first and the prophets after him, knew that the Highest Good could never be expressed in words. But they wrote that inasmuch as God revealed himself to those who were worthy and fit, he had been seen by Abraham, Isaac and Jacob. Yet what his nature, whence he came, in what manner and form he was seen, they have left to those to investigate who can become like the people who saw Him. Now he was seen not by their physical eyes but by their pure hearts: according to our Lord "Blessed are the pure in heart for they shall see God" [Mt 5:8].

VI.13[11]... Divine Wisdom then is different from faith and is the first of what are called the "gifts" (*charismata*) of God. Second to this is what we call knowledge (*gnosis*), given to those who possess clear understanding. Third comes faith (*pistis*) since the simpleminded too must be saved, arriving, as best they can, at the fear of God. Hence Paul says, "Through the Spirit one is given the word of wisdom, another, according to the same Spirit, is given the word of knowledge, to yet another faith in the same Spirit" [I Cor. 12:8-9]. So you would discover that not just anyone who happens along has received the divine Wisdom, but those receive it who are superior to and

[10]Text: SC 147.184.
[11]Text: SC 147.208.

more distinguished than the common adherents to Christianity. It is not to the lowly, the uninstructed or the uneducated that one expounds the "deep things of God."

VI.18[12] I have undertaken to offer these few of many such thoughts about God which have been entertained by holy men to show that the sacred writings of the Prophets are more noble than those Platonic sayings admired by Celsus, at least for those who have eyes able to see the majesty of Scripture.

VI.7[13] Much else might be found in Moses and the prophets. And they are older than not only Plato, but Homer too, and even the invention of writing in Greece. Our writings are worthy of the grace of God they bear and are filled with a largeness of thought. Nor have our writers, as Celsus thinks, borrowed from Plato. How would they have heeded one who did not yet exist? ... Now Celsus cites another statement of Plato to the effect that "illumination comes to those who use his method of question and answer." Well then, let us show from the Holy Scriptures that the divine Word urges us to the use of dialectic. Solomon somewhere says "Education without the process of questioning misses the mark" [Prov 10:17]. Somewhere else Jesus the Son of Sirach, in his book called *Wisdom*, says "Unexamined statements are the knowledge of a fool" [Wisdom 21:18]. We rather are familiar with the method of cross-examination since we have learned that he who has charge over the Word must be able to refute those who oppose it. If some are slack and do not train themselves to pay attention to the reading of the Scriptures or to "search them out," nor seek to understand them or to ask God about them, as Jesus commanded, and to knock on the door of their hidden mysteries, the Scriptures are not on this account devoid of wisdom.

[12]Text: SC 147.222.
[13]Text: SC 147.192.

Tertullian, Apology

Nowhere is the sharp contrast between Christian and pagan culture drawn more forcefully than in Tertullian's magnificent *Apology* (197 A.D.). The work is magnificent for the strength of its artistic design, for its economy of statement, and its rhetorical power. While these formal features are integral to the message of the *Apology* we cannot explore them ʜere. We must limit ourselves to a few central themes in the message.

Like Justin's *Apology* from which it borrows much, this work is written to rulers and its occasion is the unjust trial of Christians. It is a treatise, therefore, in defense of the Christians. As with Justin, Tertullian, too, sees the trial as a symbol of pagan perversion, stemming from a blindness induced by the demons. But Tertullian works out the social implications of the symbol much more relentlessly than Justin had done. Tertullian's *Apology* does not merely proclaim a Christian literary culture superior in its simplicity and transforming power to the proud artistic achievement of the pagans. It attacks the entire way of life of the pagans as a background for a portrait of the Christian way of life. And at the root of the two different ways of life is a false and a true knowledge of God.

At three crucial points in the *Apology* Tertullian reveals pagan society for what it is: extravagant, cruel, destructive, torn by hatreds and rebellions. Before he undertakes to answer the charges commonly raised against Christians, charges of immorality, atheism, and disloyalty, he tackles as a preliminary step the problem of the law: the law is that Christians shall not exist; discussion is therefore irrelevant. But what is the Roman attitude to law and tradition? Tertullian makes a scathing denunciation of Roman disregard for law and tradition in an exposé of Roman extravagance and sensuality:

> VI.[14] I should now like those most religious guardians
> and avengers of the laws and institutions of our fathers to

[14]Text: CCL 1.96.

reply on the question of their own faithful respect and devotion to the decrees of their ancestors. Have they never departed from any detail, never deviated at all, never struck down rules most suitable to and necessary for a disciplined moral life? Where now are those laws which restrained extravagance and display, which...forbade more than one hen—and not a fat one at that—to be set on the table...which pulled down theatres, those haunts of debauchery, even while they were rising...No distinction remains between the dress of ladies and prostitutes. With regard to women, even those ancient customs have perished which gave support to modesty and sobriety...Where is that happiness in marriage, favored no doubt by high moral standards, whereby not a single woman for almost 600 years after the founding of the city demanded a divorce? Now among women every limb is laden with gold, no lip is free from wine, and they long for divorce as though it were the proper fruit of marriage... In dress, in food, in manner of life, in manner of thought, in your very speech you have rejected your ancestors.

In the Defense proper, Tertullian takes up first the charge of incest and cannibalism, rumors which arose from the "love feasts" of the Christians and their celebration of the Eucharist at which they consumed the "Body and Blood" of Christ. He hurls back the charge at the pagans. They can imagine such unlikely deeds only because they themselves are guilty of them. He recalls the pagan's cruel practice of the "Moloch," the gladiatorial and beast fights of the amphitheatre, abortion and exposure and the frequency of incest among pagans.

IX.2[15] In Africa, children were sacrificed to Saturn as recently as the proconsulship of Tiberius... Since Saturn did not spare his own sons, obviously he would not spare

[15]Text: CCL 1.102.

the sons of others, whom indeed their own parents offered, quite willing to respond and to caress their infants to prevent them from crying at their own sacrifice... Even in that most religious city of the pious descendants of Aeneas, there is a certain Jupiter whom they wash with human blood at their own games. "But," you say, "it is the blood of a criminal who has fought with the beasts." But for that reason, no less human, I should think, or no less worse because from a criminal. In any case, it is shed in murder... How many of those who stand about thirsting for Christian blood, or even of those magistrates—so just to you, so harsh to us—shall I bring before the tribunal of their conscience for putting their own children to death? You have found only the more cruel form of death in drowning them, or exposing them to cold, or hunger, or dogs... To have an abortion is to hasten the murder, for there is no difference between destroying a life once born and terminating the life of the still unborn... Moreover, who are the incestuous more than those whom Jupiter himself has taught?

Throughout this lengthy chapter, as at the beginning and end of our excerpt, Tertullian makes his message clear: it is the mistaken understanding of the gods that leads to these terrible scenes of cruelty and passion in pagan life.

If Tertullian's strictures against pagan society begin with scenes from domestic life, they find a climax in his portrait of political and social life. Here, too, the pagan is shown to be the destructive element in society. Tertullian recounts the record of revolt in Rome. This was, in his day, not merely a matter of academic history; treason was fresh in the memory of all adults: Commodus strangled in 192, Pertinax struck down and beheaded in 193, and within the current principate of Septimius Severus, two generals, Niger in Syria and Albinus in Britain, had challenged the supremacy of the Emperor. Moreover, the practice of each newly installed emperor of giving donatives (money gifts) to the populace could encourage a hidden hope among the masses for revolution.

XXXV.6[16] I challenge the citizens of Rome itself and the servile populace of the Seven Hills: has the Roman tongue ever spared a Caesar? The Tiber is witness, and the training schools for the beast-fighters. If nature had hidden away in the human breast a sort of mirror to reflect the inner thoughts, whose heart would not reveal the expectation of one Caesar after another presiding at the distribution of the donative, even while they shout their loyalty with "May Jupiter take years from us to give to you"! This a Christian does not know to say, just as he does not know to desire another Caesar.

"But that's the common crowd" you say. Maybe, but Romans nevertheless, nor do any more insistently demand punishment for the Christians than the crowd. The higher classes, to be sure, are sincerely religious because of the authority of their position: no hostile winds from the senate, from the knights, from army, from palace officials! Whence a Cassius? a Niger? an Albinus? Whence those who attacked Caesar [Commodus] between the two laurel trees? Whence those who practiced wrestling to strangle him? Whence those who broke into the palace armed [to slay Pertinax]?

Tertullian also points an accusing finger at the economy maintained by pagan life. Responding to the charges that the Christian way of life jeopardizes the standard sources of revenue, he rails against the common practice of tax evasion, and insinuates that the pagan economy, the Gross National Product, is bloated with wealth obtained in ways which destroy the fabric of society.

XLII.9[17] "But the other revenues are threatened." Well, they should thank Christians for faithfully paying their taxes, since we do not cheat others of what is theirs. So if one should consider the loss to the treasury incurred by the false declaration of your assets, it would be easy to see that the loss from us you complain of is compensated

[16]Text: CCL 1.145.
[17]Text: CCL 1.158.

by the certainty of other revenues. XLIII. I will admit, of course, that some perhaps might legitimately complain about the sterility of Christians, first of all, pimps, seducers, harlots' attendants; then assassins, poisoners, sorcerers, as also diviners, soothsayers, and astrologers. It is highly productive to be unproductive in these ways!

Against this dark background of pagan life, Tertullian portrays in one luminous chapter the character of Christian society. We recognize in the chapter the feature, typical of the Defense speech, of defining the Christians. But for Tertullian this feature becomes a central aspect of his message. The Christian community is defined as a model society; the message is therefore a social message: Christianity offers not only salvation in light of a coming Judgment, but redemption from the corruption of an evil society. It is truly a "saving" faith.

XXXIX.1[18] I shall myself now describe the activities of the Christian sect, so that just as I have disproved the evil things said about us, I might set forth the good if I disclose the truth.

We are a body bound together by an understanding of religion, a unity of discipline, and a common hope. We come together in assembly to approach God with prayers like a band of conspirators, for God loves this kind of violence. We pray for the emperors, their ministers and magistrates, for the state of the world, for a tranquil life, for the delay of the end. We come together to consider the Sacred Writings, if current events require interpretation or suggest forewarning. With the holy words we nourish faith, confirm hope, establish confidence, and no less by the inculcation of our teachings do we strengthen discipline. At our meetings you would also find admonition, chastisement, and godly judgment; for we regard judgment to be a most serious matter knowing well that God sees all, and it is a powerful precedent of the Judgment to

[18]Text: CCL 1.150.

come, when, as a result of sin, someone is banished from our midst no longer to share with us speech, assembly or any holy rite.

Elders, well-regarded, preside over the congregation, an honor they gain not with money but through the witness of their lives, for the things of God are not for sale. We have indeed a kind of money-chest, but it is maintained not by fees as though we purchased our religion. Each one brings a small contribution on the appointed day of the month, or whenever he wishes, and only if he wishes and is able. No one is compelled, each gives of his own accord. These gifts comprise the "trust-fund," as it were, of piety. This, you will want to know, does not pay for lavish feasts, nor drinking parties, nor gluttonous revels, but goes to feeding the poor, and to burying them, to boys and girls deprived of parents and wealth, to servants too old to work, to the shipwrecked, and to those in the mines, in labor camps, or in prison who, through their confession, have become dependents of the church of God.

But in the eyes of some, deeds of a love so great serve to brand us: "Look," they say, "how the Christians love one another"—for *they* hate one other—"and how ready they are to die for their fellows!"—while *they* are more ready to kill. They go quite mad when they hear us called by the term "brothers" for no other reason, I suspect, than that with them a term of blood-relationship conceals a mere pretense of affection. We are even your brothers since we have nature as a common mother, though you, as bad brothers, are scarcely men at all. How much more worthily are those called and regarded as brothers who acknowledge God as their common Father, who drink in one common spirit of holiness, (cf. 1 Cor 12:13) who have with trembling emerged from a single womb of ignorance into the common light of truth. Perhaps we are regarded as less than legitimate because our brotherhood is not material for the tragic stage, or because we are brothers through sharing the family property—which among you usually destroys fraternal relationships. We who share mind and soul do not hesitate to share our substance. With us all things are shared except our wives. We abandon the principle of "community of goods" precisely in the one place where other men practice it: they not only steal the rights of marriage from their friends but with perfect equanimity offer them their own wives...

The Christian Love Feast

What wonder, then, if such great love is celebrated by a feast? Our modest common meals you also attack not only as the rumored occasion of crime, but also as extravagant...Our "feast" reveals its character from its name—the love known among the Greeks as "honorable affection." Whatever the expense, it is a gain to spend in the cause of piety, since we serve the poor and hungry with that refreshment...

If our feast has an honorable purpose, judge the rest of our religious rites from their purpose too. The duties of religion admit no considerations of personal advantage, admit nothing immoral. No one comes to the table before savoring a prayer to God; we eat until our hunger is satisfied and drink what befits modesty. We feast as those who remember that they must worship God throughout the night; we converse as those who know that God is listening. After our hands have been washed and the lights lit, each one is invited to come forth and sing to God, whether something from the Holy Scriptures or of his own composition according to his ability—a good indication of how much he has drunk! As it began, so the feast concludes with prayer. Then all depart, not to join bands of hoodlums or vagabonds, not for enterprises of lust, but to observe sobriety and modesty, as those who have enjoyed not so much a feast as a training in discipline.

This assembly of Christians ought to be illegal if it has anything in common with the illegal, it ought to be condemned if it is like the things that are condemned, if anyone can accuse it of having the character of a dangerous political party. Have we ever met together to plot mischief against anyone? We are when assembled what we are when scattered, the same as a body as we are individuals: we harm no one, we injure no one. When the upright and the good assemble, when the pious and the chaste come together, you have not what can be called a "party," but a "senate."

The message that Christians were a redemptive leaven in society provided an obvious context for a refutation of the pagan fear that disasters came to the state as a punishment from angry gods for the neglect of their worship, a neglect inspired by the Christians. Was not, the pagans argued, the greatness of Rome the direct result of their religiosity, their cultivation of the gods? Were not disasters, then, the voice of the gods calling for the extermination of Christians? Tertullian's response finds echoes down to Augustine: the Romans have succeeded as a political power in the face of the greatest disregard for the gods, and if misfortunes come from the neglect of the gods, they come from the neglect of the true God, not the Roman gods. He points to the contradiction in the Roman tradition which assigned to Numa the task of establishing religion, but only after the state had already achieved power:

> XXV.12[19] Well, then, religion advanced after the power of the state had increased. But how wrong to suppose the Roman name achieved supremacy as a reward for religiosity when religion was subsequent to power!... Indeed, how could the Romans become great through regard for religion when their greatness arose from their disregard of religion? If I am not mistaken, every kingdom, every empire is acquired through war and enlarged by victories. Wars and victories mean cities captured and usually destroyed. Now these are affairs not

[19]Text: CCL 1.137.

> without some injury to the gods: city-walls and temples
> alike are levelled, citizens and priests alike slaughtered,
> sacred and profane treasures alike plundered. Thus
> Roman sacrilege is as great as Roman power, the victo-
> ries over the gods as many as over nations, as much
> wealth from the spoils of war as images of the captive
> gods remaining to be sold.

This step in the direction of a theodicy, of justifying the
ways of God to men, of revealing the Christian God as one
not only of mercy, but of justice too, could only deepen and
enrich Christian eschatology, the doctrine of resurrection
and Judgment, which, as we have seen, was so integral a part
of the message from the earliest times. Tertullian sees the
special propriety in bringing his message to a conclusion on
this theme. First, he rounds off the pagan-Christian contrast
which dominates the *Apology* by invoking those symbols of
pagan knowledge and culture, the philosophers, as a witness
to the fact that, however erroneously, pagans themselves
have maintained doctrines something like the resurrection
and last Judgment, and therefore have no reason to scoff at
Christian naiveté. Second, the theme of "The Great Assize"
with its implacably just trial of all who have denied God's
truth and justice recalls at an effective moment the point of
departure for this *Apology*—the unjust trial of Christians.
Third, he was able to conclude by bringing the question of
theodicy directly to bear on the problem of Christian suffering, for however one might debate the question of public
disasters, the failure of their God to rescue the Christians
from suffering seemed to make nonsense of a Christian
claim that God cares for His own. The resurrection to a
glorious reward for the just who have suffered thus becomes
integral to the message. Tertullian arrests attention with a
sharp image of the millenial borderline between the worlds
of time and eternity, then portrays the final Judgment and
the Christian hope, comparing the former with those disasters commonly regarded as "divine judgments," and recalling the heed paid to pagan philosophers and poets for
similar beliefs:

XLVIII.12[20] When therefore the boundary and borderline which gapes midway has been removed, so that
the form of even that [millenial] world, still temporal
and spread like a canopy over the eternal order, disappears, then the whole human race will be restored to settle
the account of good or bad as each deserves, an account
to be paid throughout the limitless length of eternity.
Hence no death again nor resurrection, but we shall be the
same as we are now, worshippers of God, always with
God, clothed in a substance appropriate to eternity. But
the profane and those not right with God shall suffer the
penalty of a fire likewise undying, since it receives from its
own divine nature the gift of indestructibility. Philosophers know the difference between the hidden and the
common fire. The latter, for human use, is vastly different
from the former which makes its appearance as the Judgment of God—whether hurling lightning bolts from the
sky or belching forth from the earth through the tops of
the mountains. Its power to burn does not diminish, but
while it expends itself it replaces what is lost. Accordingly, the volcanoes abide although always burning, and
whoever is struck by lightning is safe so that no present
fire can reduce him to ashes. These are proofs of the
eternal fire, evidence of a Judgment continually nourishing the punishment. The mountains burn and are not
consumed; what about the guilty, and the enemies of
God? These are called presumptuous views in our case
alone; among philosophers and poets they are utmost
wisdom, the products of distinguished intelligence! They
are wise, we are fools. They are to be esteemed, we to be
ridiculed, even more, to be punished!

In his final words Tertullian answers the question of Christian suffering:

L.11[21] . . . And yet [you say] whoever hopes for this true
resurrection from God is mad if he suffers for God. 12.

[20]Text: CCL 1.167.
[21]Text: CCL 1.171.

Proceed, good magistrates! The people will love you more if you sacrifice the Christians for them. Torture us, stretch us on the rack, condemn us, destroy us: your injustice is proof of our innocence. For this reason God permits us to suffer such things... Nor yet does your cruelty however refined aid your cause. Rather, it entices people to our sect. We spring up in larger numbers, the more we are mown down and harvested by you: Christian blood is seed!... That very obstinacy which you curse becomes an instructor of others. For who in reflecting upon it is not forced to seek what power resides within? Who when he has sought does not assent, does not desire to suffer, that he might buy up the entire grace of God, procure his own pardon by the payment of his blood. All sins are forgiven by this deed. That is why we thank you for your judgments. For there is a rivalry between things human and divine: when you condemn, God pardons!

Origen, Against Celsus

The emphatic threat of punishment for unbelievers must strike the modern reader as a harsh and jarring note on which to conclude what has been a clear effort to lead to faith. We pause therefore to note that some Christians regarded the threat as an effective instrument of persuasion and for that reason important to the message. In his third book *Against Celsus* Origen justifies this method. He points to its effect upon a certain class of people:

III.78[22]... These, stirred by the fear of the punishments which have been announced, and encouraged to desist from conduct which merits punishment, endeavor to devote themselves to piety according to the Christian way. They become so taken with the Word, in fear of the everlasting punishments named through the Word, that they despise every torture devised by men against many sufferings.

[22]Text: SC 136.176.

He compares the rigorous Solon to the "father of Christian teaching":

> III.79[23] . . . Thus the father of Christian teaching might say: "I gave the best laws and the teaching which the many could sustain for the improvement of their morals. And those who sin I have threatened with punishment and sufferings not at all imaginary, but true and inevitable, designed to lead to repentance those who resist, even though they do not understand my intent in punishing or the purpose of the sufferings."

Later he argues that when unbelievers are recalcitrant and refuse the message delivered by gentle discourse, then Christians have a responsibility to persuade them perforce by the threat of punishment:

> VIII.52.[24] Since we have been persuaded by countless proofs to live our lives according to the Christian faith, it is our chief desire that all others should, so far as possible, make their own the teachings of Christianity. But wherever we find those who are prejudiced as a result of slander against the Christians, who wrongly believe that Christians are impious people and who will therefore not listen to us who say we are teachers of a sacred doctrine, then out of concern for their welfare we undertake as far as possible to portray vividly the teaching about the eternal punishment upon the ungodly, and so make even those who are unwilling to become Christians receive the word.

Here, in theory at least, we are only a step away from the view accepted a century and a half later, when Christianity had achieved political supremacy, that inducements of deprivation and persecution, should be applied to Jews, heretics and pagans to force them to accept the message.

---

[23]Text: SC 136.178.
[24]Text: SC 150.288.

Minucius Felix, Octavius

It is in a very different vein that the *Octavius* of Minucius Felix was written, and it is appropriate to consider it here since its main interest for us lies in what appears to be its affirmation of a reasoned and philosophical method in presenting the message to pagans. It is closely related to Tertullian's *Apology* as its many parallels in content prove. Most scholars now agree that the *Octavius* is the later of the two, and it is probable that it was intended to form a contrast with the flamboyant forensic approach of Tertullian in presenting the message.

That the *Octavius* is deeply interested in the problems of methodology, that is, of how to present the gospel to pagans, emerges from several striking paragraphs in the work. Minucius sets the scene carefully: Minucius, with two friends—Octavius, a Christian, and Caecilius, a cultivated pagan—are walking from Rome to Ostia when Caecilius presses a kiss upon a statue of Serapis. Octavius is surprised that his friend Minucius (also called Marcus) has been a close neighbor of Caecilius and has failed to communicate the Christian message:

> III.[25] Then Octavius said, "It is not the part of a good man, Marcus, my brother, to leave a companion so close to you both at home and abroad in the darkness of common superstition and to allow him in broad daylight to stumble over stones, even though carved and anointed and wreathed. You must know that the disgrace of this error falls no less upon you than upon him.

If this brief passage serves to remind us of the expectation of daily witness which we have observed in Chapter 1, we cannot at the same time miss the suggestion that what follows in the work is concerned with a question about presenting the message.

As a result of Octavius' concern, the friends agree to hold

[25]Text: LCL, ed. Rendall, 316.

a formal debate in the philosophical manner. Caecilius as a pagan will argue for the pagan belief and practice, Octavius will defend the Christian cause, Minucius, though a Christian, will play the part of impartial arbiter of the debate. Again, the author stresses method when he has Caecilius comment on the rigors of the philosophical mode:

> IV[26]... This is a matter entirely for Octavius and me. If he agrees to debate with me, a devoted pagan, he will soon discover that it is much easier merely to converse among friends than to undertake now a philosophical debate.

Since the pagan Caecilius speaks first, he determines the topics for debate and thus shapes Octavius' message. These are topics appropriate to philosophical discussion: the existence and knowledge of God, the place of religion in social and political life, the question of theodicy, and the legitimacy of the grounds of suspicion entertained by pagans against the Christians. Octavius, in his speech, responds to these themes. Accordingly, there is not a word about Christ, and virtually nothing about the Scriptures. In the end, the result is, not a full Christian conversion, but a recognition of error on the part of Caecilius and of the need to be instructed in the Christian faith:

> XL.[27] While I was silently reflecting on these things, Caecilius broke in: "I congratulate my Octavius ever so warmly, and myself too, nor do I await your judgment. We have won on these terms: though beaten, I claim a victory. For just as he is my victor, so I enjoy a triumph over error. On the main points, therefore, I confess Providence. I grant his view of God, and I agree about the good will of the sect I now take as my own. Yet certain matters still remain, not in contradiction to the truth, but essential for full instruction. Since the day is drawing to a close, we shall tomorrow consider these the more readily as we hope to find complete agreement."

[26]Text: LCL 320.
[27]Text: LCL. 434.

Octavius is ready for the catechumenate. It has been possible by the sheer power of philosophical discourse to convince a pagan of the truth of the Christian message about God, his justice, and his judgment, but the distinctive truths of the mysteries of the faith remain to be divulged.

We have seen that from the earliest times recorded in Acts, the appeal to pagan culture has been an integral part of the Exhortation. Minucius carries the principle to its extreme limit: the entire presentation is made within the terms established by pagan philosophy. A highly positive view of the possibilities of philosophical discourse for proclaiming the message is implied: it can not only remove errors but lead to a recognition of Christian truth about God and His world, and to the desire for conversion, though it cannot—and should not—touch the mysteries of Christian faith. Moreover, we are probably intended to understand that this is the *ideal* way to present the message to pagans. The *Octavius* offers a norm for Christian witness: one should endeavor to lead an unbeliever to the point of faith through general revelation, through natural reason. Only then is the pagan mind and heart, no longer profane, ready to hear and understand the core of the Christian message. In essence, the position is not so different from that of Justin suggested in his *Dialogue with Trypho*, but where Justin presented the limits of philosophical discourse in a negative light (it could demolish cherished views, but could not lead to truth) Octavius sees those limits positively as the borderline of faith.

As I have indicated, in content the work of Minucius is highly derivative and there is little that is fresh in the Christian themes he expounds. But there is a new prominence here given to the question of theodicy which may well reflect a growing pagan fear of the dangers of Christianity to the welfare of the State. Caecilius had pled for the traditional religion on the familiar grounds that Roman power was the result of Roman religiosity. Octavius assaults the position:

25[28]. . . That primitive people [the Romans] assembled

[28]Text: LCL. 388.

at Asylum[29]: there flocked together the profligates, criminals, incestuous, assassins, traitors, while Romulus himself, the ruler and commander, in order to exceed the crimes of his people, murdered his brother. These are the first beginnings of a religious state! Then, without precedent the people carried off maidens already engaged to others, already given, and even some women now married, violated them, made sport of them, went to war with their parents, that is their fathers-in-law, and so shed the blood of relatives. What can be more irreligious, what more presumptuous, what more confident in the very boldness of the crime? Other kings and subsequent leaders shared with Romulus a common way of life: to expel their neighbors from their lands, to overthrow nearby cities along with their temples and altars, to take their peoples captive, to achieve greatness at the expense of others and by their own crimes.

Thus, whatever the Romans hold, occupy, possess is the fruit of insolence: all their temples are built from the sale of spoils, that is, from the devastation of cities, from plundering the gods, from the slaughter of priests. To serve gods that have been conquered, to worship those you have overcome, this is insolence, this true insult. For to worship what you have taken by force is to hallow sacrilege, not to honor the divine powers. Hence the Romans sinned as often as they triumphed, they spoiled the gods as often as they conquered nations. And so the Romans became great not because they were religious but because their sacrilege went unpunished. Nor were they able to have as their helpers in war the gods against whom they had taken arms. Yet they began to worship those gods they had humiliated by defeat. How could those gods help the Romans who could offer no help to their own people against Roman arms?

As with Tertullian, so in the *Octavius* the phenomenon of Christian suffering demanded explanation. But the problem

---

[29]Asylum: the place where Romulus promised the refugees sanctuary.

here is larger than simply the suffering in persecution. Poverty, disease, misfortune, are sufferings common to all, but are they not inappropriate to those who live in the favor of God? To this question Minucius' response is that of a Christian securely domiciled in his world, less eschatological therefore, and more ethical than Tertullian's solution to the problem of suffering.

> 36[30] . . . That most of us are called poor is not our disgrace but our glory. For just as the soul is weakened by luxury, so it is made strong by frugality. Yet who can be poor who has no need, who has no desire for the possessions of another, who is rich towards God? . . . We feel and suffer, it is true, the normal afflictions of the body, but this is not a punishment, it is our "military training." Courage grows strong through weakness, and disaster is often a school for virtue, while strength of body and mind slackens without the exercise of labor . . . Accordingly, God is not unable to help us nor does he disregard us, since he controls all things and loves his own, but through adversities, he tests and examines each one, through dangers he determines the character of individuals, and to the very point of death he searches the will of a man, knowing well that nothing can be lost. As gold is tried by fire, so are we by the troubles that beset us.

Tertullian, To Scapula

The message of divine wrath and judgment on a world which has abandoned God took a new form in two letters written in the first half of the third century, one to a proconsul, the other to a government official. Again, both presuppose a pagan complaint that disasters come upon the State as a punishment for the Christian disregard of the ancient religion. Tertullian addressed a letter to the governor Scapula and turned the tables on the pagans:

[30]Text: LCL. 424.

III.[31] And yet, as we said above, we must grieve because
no state will shed our blood with impunity. Thus under
Hilarian the governor, in regard to our burial places,
after the people had shouted "No fields for burial," they
themselves had no fields for threshing, for they had no
harvest. It has become clear of what the rains of the past
year should remind the human race—that flood which
occurred long ago as a result of man's unbelief and sin.
And the fires which recently hung over the walls of Carthage by night, those who saw them know what they
portend; and what message the earlier thunderings
roared, they know who endured them. All these are signs
of the approaching wrath of God, a wrath we must in
every possible way announce and proclaim, and pray
meanwhile that the anticipatory disasters be only local.

It is apparent at once that these words are more than a
retorsion of the pagan complaint. Tertullian's message conveys his sense of salvation-history as a divine pattern of
events anticipated and fulfilled. The present evils reveal God
the judge at work in our world, which signals his justice and
power on the Day of Judgment.

Cyprian, To Demetrianus

Almost half a century later Cyprian addressed a similar
letter to Demetrianus, a government official. It shares with
Tertullian's letter *To Scapula* a tone of impatience. Cyprian
sets the letter in the context of a long effort on his part to
persuade Demetrianus of the truth of the Christian message.
That effort, he says, he has now abandoned for it is an
"ineffectual labor" to discourse to a deaf man. Yet everywhere the charge is being raised that the ills of the state are
due to Christians:

[31]Text: CCL 2.1129.

2[32] But when you say that many are blaming us because wars arise more frequently, because plague and famine rage, because clear skies have long prevented rain-storms and showers, it is time to speak.

In response, Cyprian's message is, like Tertullian's, one of impending judgment, of which the present disasters are an anticipation, simple justice for the pagan refusal to worship the true God:

5.[33] That wars follow more closely one after another, that sterility and hunger compound our woes, that diseases rage and health fails, that the human race is devastated by plague, from all this you should learn what has been predicted, that in the last times evils and suffering would abound, and as the Day of Judgment now approaches the severity of an angry God burns ever more intensely for the punishment of the human race. For these events do not occur, as your false complaints and foolish ignorance of the truth charge, because your gods are not worshipped by us, but rather because the true God is not worshipped by you. Since He is the Lord and ruler of the world and all things are governed by his will and consent, nothing can happen which he himself has not done or permitted. Therefore when those events occur which point to the anger of an indignant God, we are not responsible who worship God. They are inflicted rather because of your sins, since you neither seek God nor fear him, nor lay aside your superstition nor come to know true religion. They are inflicted so that he who is the one God over all might alone be worshipped and sought by all.

There is nothing fresh in Cyprian's message. Its importance for us lies in the growing urgency of the problem, and the determination of Christians to use the occasion to preach unashamedly a message of repentance, or punishment.

[32]Text: CCL 3A.35.
[33]Text: CCL 3A.37.

Suggestions for Further Reading

Baylis, H.J., *Minucius Felix and His Place among the Early Fathers of the Latin Church*, London 1928.

An old book which discusses the literary-critical problems of the *Octavius*, but has a good chapter (5) on "The Objectives of Minucius."

Chadwick, H., *Early Christian Thought and the Classical Tradition*, Oxford 1966.

Chadwick shows how Justin, Clement and Origen shaped their message to take advantage of the heritage of classical philosophy.

Clarke, C.W. (tr.), *The Octavius of Minucius Felix*, New York 1974.

In an excellent introduction of 50 pages, Clarke analyzes the reasons why Minucius' message took the form of the philosophical dialogue.

Daniélou, J., *Origen*. Trans. Walter Mitchell, New York 1955.

Chapter 5 is devoted to a discussion of *Against Celsus*, showing how Origen distinguished the Christian message from philosophy.

Sage, M., *Cyprian*, Cambridge, MA 1975.

A general study of Cyprian.

Sider, R. D., "On Symmetrical Composition in Tertullian" JTS (1973).

Largely an analysis from a rhetorical and theological point of view of Tertullian's *Apology*.

Chapter Five

THE MESSAGE TO
THE PAGANS III

We cannot have an adequate grasp of the Christian message to pagans until we have considered what are perhaps its two greatest literary embodiments, the *Divine Institutes* of Lactantius and Augustine's *City of God*. These works also demand our attention because they each appear at a period of radical change in the Roman Empire resulting in an adjustment in the relations between pagans and Christians. Lactantius' work seems to have been begun during the last persecution of Christians in the early fourth century, but was finished only when Constantine had assumed power and established freedom of religion, at least in the West. Augustine wrote a century later. In the course of that century, not only did Christianity establish itself as the religion of the Emperors, but paganism was put on the defensive by a series of imperial decrees, notably those of 391 and 392. Nevertheless, paganism showed a remarkable resilience, and when, less than 20 years after the decrees of 391 and 392, Rome fell to the barbarian Alaric, paganism was quick to lay the blame upon the forced desertion of the ancient religion. It was in this context that Augustine delivered the message of the *City of God* to the pagans. Finally, both of these works offer Christianity as a way of life, indeed, a culture, and do so with an explication more massive and thorough than anything attempted before in literature directed to pagans.

Lactantius, Institutes:
The Message as a Christian Philosophy

The work of Lactantius holds a special interest for us for two reasons. First, it presents Christian faith as a complete way of life explicable by a coherent and integrated system of thought. Second, the work betrays persistent and intense reflection on the problems of methodology—how to present the message to the pagans. These two aspects of Lactantius' work are not always distinct. For example, the intellectual structure he builds, as we shall see, is itself a methodological affirmation. Sometimes, however, he addresses the problem of method quite explicitly.

We may begin with the statement of intention and the discussion of methods, remarkably full and clear, in the first chapters of Book V. This statement of his own purpose and the problems encountered by his predecessors in presenting the message to pagans requires a lengthy extract.

> V.1[1] If any devout pagan, still sadly enthralled by a profound superstition, should come upon this work of ours, in which I affirm the one Creator of the world, the Controller of its enormous structure, I have no doubt that he will attack it with curses, and almost before reading will abuse it, cast it away, utter imprecations upon it. And if he allows himself to read the book, or to hear it read, he will think himself defiled, and guilty of an inexpiable crime. Yet I should like to ask that in accordance with common human rights he does not condemn before he has heard the story out. If the sacrilegious, if traitors, if *venefici* sorcerers have the right to defend themselves, then no one ought to be condemned before the case has been investigated. It is appropriate therefore

[1]Text: CSEL 19.398.

to ask that if anyone picks up this book and reads, observes, listens, he should defer judgment to the end.

This request, however, we shall never be granted, for I am quite aware of human pertinacity. Our enemies fear that we shall overcome, and they will be forced at last by the resounding claims of truth, to surrender. They therefore raise a clamor and interrupt to prevent themselves from hearing; they shut their eyes to prevent themselves from seeing what we offer them. In this, of course, they reveal a loss of confidence in their own perverted reason, since they are unwilling to learn, while they do not dare to debate because they know they can easily be defeated. Hence there is no discussion, and as Ennius says; "wisdom is driven from our midst, violence determines our affairs" [*Annals* VIII fr. 2]. Since they are eager to condemn as guilty those whom they certainly know are innocent, they are unwilling to investigate their plea of innocence—as though it were a greater injustice to condemn an innocence once proven than to condemn an innocence never confirmed. They fear that if they should hear our case, they would not be able to condemn us.

This is why they torture, slay, exterminate the worshippers of the supreme God, that is, the just. Nor are those who hate so savagely able to explain their hatred. Because they themselves have gone astray, they are angry at those who follow the true path, and though they could correct themselves they only add to their error by their cruel deeds. They defile themselves with innocent blood, they wrench souls dedicated to God away from the bodies they have lacerated. With such now I undertake to engage in debate; and to lead to the truth from their foolish ways those who have more readily thirsted for blood than for the words of the just.

Will it be a lost cause? By no means! For if we are unable to save them from the death to which they madly rush, or to summon back to light and life from error's path those who resist their own salvation, still we can bring strength to our own people whose convictions are not firm and fixed and deeply rooted. Indeed, many waver, and especially those who read, for philosophers, orators, and poets are deadly dangerous since they are easily able to snare unsuspecting souls with the sweetness of their speech, with the soft music of their poetry. This is the honey that coats the poison. For this reason I wish to unite philosophy and religion that the foolish teaching of paganism should present no dangers to the studious, and that henceforth a knowledge of the liberal arts should not only not harm the cause of religion and justice, but actually help it to a great extent, if the teacher is more disciplined in virtue, and wiser in the truth. Finally, I at least, if no others, shall reap some benefit. My conscience will take delight, my mind rejoice thus bathing in the light of truth. This is the nourishment of the soul, which we take with marvellous pleasure.

Still, one must not give up. Perhaps we "do not speak to the deaf" [Vergil, *Eclogues* 10.8]. For our times are not so bad that you cannot find some people with sound minds who will delight in the truth and, when the right path has been revealed, will recognize it and follow. But the cup must be sweetened with the heavenly honey of philosophy, so that the unsuspecting can drink the bitter remedies without aversion. The sweetness will at once entice and hide the harsh and bitter flavor with its pleasant taste. It is, above all, because the prophets spoke simple and everyday language (for they were addressing the common people), that the wise and learned, and the rulers of this world place no confidence in the Holy Scriptures. The Scriptures are despised by those who refuse to hear or read anything but what is polished and refined. Nothing sticks in their heads, unless it has flattered their ears with its soothing sound. What seems plain and lowly, they consider vulgar and silly, stuff for old wives' tales. They think nothing can be true which is not also pleasant to hear, nothing trustworthy which does not bring delight; no one judges a thing by its truth, but by its adornment. Therefore they do not believe the divine truths, because these are free from all cosmetics, nor do they believe those who expound them since these too are either completely uneducated or only modestly learned. Rarely are they eloquent, and with good reason, for eloquence is a servant of the world. It displays itself before the people, happy to please in an evil cause; indeed, it often tries to fight against the truth just to show its strength. It seeks wealth, desires honor, demands the highest rank. It looks down upon our truth as something low, flees things hidden as quite contrary to itself. It rejoices in publicity, desires crowds and celebrity. This is why wisdom and truth lack suitable messengers. And if by chance any cultured persons have devoted themselves to it, they have failed to give an adequate defense.

Of those I know, Minucius Felix deserves a distinguished place among its advocates. His book, the *Octavius*, shows what a fine defender of the truth he would have been if he had devoted himself entirely to the task. Tertullian, also, was deeply learned in every kind of literature, but his style is difficult, unembellished, and very obscure. He accordingly has won little fame. Cyprian alone therefore has stood out distinguished above the rest both because he had gained great glory from his profession as an orator, and because he wrote much that can be admired in its own *genre*. His mind was quick, fertile, sweet, and clear (and clarity is the greatest virtue of speech), so you could never tell which was his greatest strength: whether readiness of speech, clarity in explanation, or force in persuasion. Yet he cannot satisfy those who know nothing, apart from his words, about the mystery of faith, since he spoke mystical truths designed only for the faithful. Consequently, when educated pagans come to know his work, they usually laugh at him. I have heard that someone rather cleverly changed one letter in his name and called him Coprian [buffoon], as though a man of exceptional ability, quite capable of better things, had taken himself to cheap and worthless tales. But if this is the case with him, whose eloquence is not unpleasant, what must we think of those whose style is dry and disagreeable? They could have had no force of persuasion, no precision in proof, no sharpness at all in refutation...

V.4.[2] When those I have mentioned had expounded their own profane literature in my presence and to my grief, I was moved to undertake this work by their proud impiety, by my knowledge of the truth, and, I believe, by God, so that I might refute with all the force at my command the plaintiffs against justice. I do not write against those who could be crushed with a few words; I wish rather to put an end with one single blow to all who everywhere undertake or will undertake the accuser's role. I know that many people in many places—and not only among the Greeks but among the Latins, too—have with their writings built a monument to injustice. Since I could not respond to each individually, I thought I should defend my case by overthrowing our earlier opponents with all their writings, and from those yet to come, cut away every opportunity to write or to reply. If only they will listen, I shall certainly accomplish this, that whoever becomes acquainted with our truth will either accept as his own what he formerly condemned, or, next best, will at last stop scoffing.

Tertullian, it is true, made a full defense of our case in his *Apology*. However, it is one thing to reply to accusers, where the task is defense or denial alone; quite another to instruct, as I wish to do, in a way which embraces the entire system of our teaching. I have not avoided this labor, for I have wanted to complete the case Cyprian left unfinished when he tried to answer Demetrian who, as he himself says, was railing and clamoring against the truth. Cyprian, however, did not argue his case as he should have. For Demetrian should have been refuted by rational arguments and proofs, not by quoting Scripture which he regarded as quite false, fictitious and contrived. Since Cyprian was arguing against a man ignorant of the truth, he should not have introduced him at once to the

[2]Text: CSEL 19.411.

Holy Scriptures, but should have instructed him as a beginner, then gradually have shown him the elements of the light, and thus not blind him with too much brightness at once. An infant cannot digest solid food and strong meat, but is nourished with milk and soft foods; then when it has grown stronger, it can take a more adult diet. So in the case of Demetrian, since he was not yet able to receive the divine words, he should first have been offered human witnesses, those of the philosophers and historians, and thus be refuted as far as possible by his own pagan authors. But this was not Cyprian's mode, for he was carried away by his enormous knowledge of the Holy Scriptures and was satisfied only with those things on which our faith rests. Therefore I have undertaken, by the help of God, to present the case properly, and at the same time provide a way for others to follow. And if, through our message, learned and eloquent men begin to turn this way, and choose to display their abilities and their power of speech in the field of truth, no one can doubt that false religions will soon disappear, and all worldly philosophy perish, for all will be persuaded that this is the only religion, the only true wisdom. But I have digressed further than I intended.

Two points may be noted. First, Lactantius' language clarifies for us the audience to which he directs his message. It is first of all a pagan audience, but he also knows that Christians will read his work, and he has written for their benefit as well. We see here again the firm belief that a message to pagans could also be a message of confirmation and edification to Christians. In the second place, insofar as Lactantius' audience is the pagan of the early fourth century, it is above all the educated pagan, and this has deeply affected the presentation of his message. He is determined to present the message in polished language, bringing to bear upon it as far as possible the resources of pagan culture. It is for the same reason that he undertakes to present Christianity as a total "system," a system whose structure is explained by the cadres of classical philosophy. Indeed, the *Divine*

Institutes forms a sort of "Christian commentary" on classical philosophy. Yet he brings to his discussion not only the pagan inheritance of philosophy, but in addition the classical tradition of rhetoric, especially at those points where it could contribute, by the empirical methods of investigation it had acquired in the courts, to the evidence for the Christian faith. To a considerable extent, the forensic power of Tertullian and the sweet philosophical reasonableness of Minucius Felix are brought together in Lactantius, though his work far outreaches either of theirs in its scope and imaginative power. To understand Lactantius' message, we must now range more widely over his work, noting especially the degree to which he follows along an intellectual path familiar to educated pagans.

We should observe first that Lactantius is highly conscious of the need to discuss the problem of faith according to accepted standards of critical methodology. Underlying all of Lactantius' thought in the *Institutes* is belief, appropriate to a philosophical perspective, in the rationality of man, and the consequent legitimacy of the use of reason for argumentation, persuasion, and the discovery of truth. Lactantius' commitment to reason becomes explicit at many points throughout the *Institutes*, nowhere perhaps more sharply than when he attacks the pagans for holding irrationally to custom:

> 11.6[3] Look! reason teaches you that the religions of the gods are not true. What will you do? Follow your traditions or follow reason?. . . If you choose reason, you must abandon the institutions and authority of your ancestors, since that alone is right which reason prescribes. But if out of piety you follow ancestral custom, then confess that they were fools who devoted themselves to religious rites devised quite contrary to reason, while you are silly to worship what you believe to be false.

The central place given to reason affects Lactantius' work in several ways. He persistently structures his argumenta-

[3]Text: CSEL 19.123.

tion upon the two kinds of evidence refined through centuries of experience in the ancient courts of law and whose strength lay in their appeal to reason: logical deduction from commonly held assumptions, and witnesses. He underlines his method at the very beginning of his work. Passing lightly over the question of Providence, he undertakes the proof of the one God first by deduction from common assumptions:

> 1.3[4] Let our work therefore begin with that question which follows and grows out of these considerations (i.e. about Providence): whether the world is ruled by the power of one God or many. Now everyone who can perceive and reflect, understands that he is one who has created all things and rules his creation by his power. For what need is there of many to maintain the governance of the world.?

After a chapter of such argument he comes to prove God's oneness of divine power by the evidence of witnesses, first (1.4) the testimony of the prophets, and then the testimony of pagan writers.

> 1.5[5] And now let us leave the witness of prophets, since proof drawn from those they disbelieve may seem inappropriate. Let us come to authors, and cite as evidence of the truth those very witnesses which they usually employ against us, that is, poets and philosophers.

But not only does Lactantius present the message of Christianity in the rational terms beloved by its cultured despisers. A critical methodology assumes that events are explicable. Consequently he seeks everywhere to explain the motivation, to give a rational account, of phenomena, and particularly of religious phenomena. Earlier apologists, too, had attempted to explain the fact of idolatry. But Lactantius sees idolatry, at one level, as a natural and human phenomenon and makes much greater efforts to explain its histori-

[4]Text: CSEL 19.7.
[5]Text: CSEL 19.11

cal and psychological roots. Accepting the theory of Euhemerus, as all the Fathers did, that the gods were dead men who had been divinized, Lactantius explains the process historically:

> 1.15.[6] And so, since it is agreed that they (the gods) were once men, we can easily see how they came to be called gods. Now there were no kings before Saturn and Uranus because so few folk, and these lived a rustic life without any ruler. There can be no doubt therefore that when kings appeared, people began to extol the king himself and his whole family with the highest praises and new honors, so that they called their king a god, either because of his astonishing power (as they, still unlettered and naive, considered it), or, more often, to flatter the power he then possessed, or because of the civilizing benefits he had bestowed upon mankind. Then when the kings died, beloved by those on whom they had imposed the settled life, their absence was sorely felt. The people therefore made likenesses of them to take comfort from looking upon their images. They went even further, and in devout appreciation of their worth, began to worship the memory of the dead. In this way, they would appear to be thankful to those who had helped them, and would also stir up in the successors of the kings a passion for good rule. Cicero says as much in his treatise *On the Nature of the Gods*: "Human experience and common custom have undertaken by general consent to exalt to heaven men distinguished by their services. So Hercules, Castor, Pollux, Aesculapius, Bacchus" [2.24.62]. Elsewhere he says: "One can see that in most states the memory of brave men has become sacred with the dignity of the immortal gods, in order to arouse virtue, and to encourage the best men to face danger more willingly for the sake of the commonwealth" [cf. *On the Nature of the Gods* 3.19.50]. It was on these grounds no doubt that the Romans consecrated their Caesars and the Moors their

[6]Text: CSEL 19.55.

kings. Thus gradually religions arose, and those who first knew the kings instilled the rituals into their children and grandchildren, whence they came to all posterity.

So also, like Cicero, Lactantius recognized the political and sociological factors which motivated those who established pagan worship: they used religion to stabilize a turbulent populace:

> 1.22[7] . . . Accordingly he (Numa) established priests, flamens, salii, augurs, and organized the gods into families. In this way he tamed the wild spirits of a young tribe and turned them from war to the pursuits of peace.

No pagan, trained in the rhetorical schools in empirical methods of investigation, in a "scientific" approach to the search for truth, would miss in this exploration of motives and of the course of events described in these two passages the claim of Lactantius that the Christian message, too, seeks to persuade on the common ground of reason. Even when Lactantius turns to theological reasons to explain idolatry, he is not content simply to attest the activity of demons. He goes on to explain the ultimate origin of evil, the source whence the demonic finds its motivation. He is explicit about his methodology:

> 11.8[8] I shall therefore offer an explanation of all these things so that obscure and different subjects may be more easily understood. I shall lay bare all the illusions in the pretence of divine power, the trickery by which people have been led to depart far from the path of truth. I shall pursue the matter in depth so that if anyone ignorant of the truth should undertake to read this book, he may be instructed and come to understand what is the root and cause of these evils. When he has seen the light, he can perceive his own error and that of the whole human race.
>
> Now God was, and always is, the fountain of full and perfect goodness, so that goodness like a stream had its

[7]Text: CSEL 19.88.
[8]Text: CSEL 19.128.

source in him and flowed out into an abundant river. Therefore, since God was most prudent in designing, most skillful in making, before ever he created this world he brought forth a Spirit like his own endowed with the powers of God the Father. Why he willed this, I shall attempt to explain in Book IV. Then he made a second spirit whose nature did not remain true to its divine origin. It was accordingly infected by its own jealousy as by a poison, and passed over from good to evil. By its own free choice—for God had given it a will which was free— it assumed a name opposed to what it was. Hence envy appears as the source of all evils. For it envied the first spirit who remained steadfast, and thus pleasing and dear to God the Father. The Greeks call it the devil who by himself became evil after being good. We call him accuser, because he accuses us before God of the sins into which he himself has enticed us.

For Lactantius, reasoned argument, rational explanation must be central in the presentation of the message to pagans.

It was a natural consequence of his emphasis on reason and his interest in the educated pagan that Lactantius endeavored to present the message as far as possible through the methods and terms of pagan philosophy. This meant, in the first instance, the development of a system analogous to that of the philosophers, where one began with basic assumptions about knowing and being, proceeded rationally to questions about behavior and on to a consideration of man's true end. Minucius Felix, too, had affirmed the utility of the philosophical method as a way of presenting the message, without, however, making any attempt to construct an all-embracing system. But for Lactantius, writing a Christian philosophy meant further that the terms of his system should be those authenticated by their antiquity. Consequently, the central terms of his message are those with a pedigree of more than half a millennium of Greek thought: wisdom, justice, virtue and the immortality of the soul. The skeleton of his system can be indicated in a few propositions: from God, the source of Being, comes true wisdom; from true wisdom comes true justice; true justice is realized in true virtue; by true virtue man gains immortality; in immortality man is led to his true end which is God. To illustrate, we shall have to be content with only a few scattered excerpts.

A. The Source of Wisdom:

> IV.3[9]...Where wisdom and religion are bound together in an inseparable union, both must be true. For in worshipping we ought to understand, that is, to know what and how we ought to worship, while in understanding we ought to worship, that is to fulfill in act and deed what we know. Where, then, is wisdom joined with religion? There, of course, where one God is worshipped, where life and every action is referred to one source, one principle. Accordingly those are "wise men" who are also priests of God...Therefore religion is contained in wisdom and wisdom in religion, and they cannot be separated. To be wise is nothing else than to honor the true God with true and reverent adoration.

B. Wisdom and Justice:

Lactantius' conception of wisdom as the source of justice is expressed best in a lengthy consideration of the apparent folly of the truly just man. Test cases are examined: in a shipwreck it would appear to be wise but not just to save yourself by taking a plank from another man; similarly, in case of need, to take a horse from a wounded man seems the part of wisdom, but not justice.

> V.17[10]...To conclude the argument: reason itself teaches that the just man cannot also be a fool, nor a wise man unjust. For he who is a fool does not know what the just and the good are, which is why he always goes astray. He is led like a captive by his vices, unable to resist, since he cannot have the virtue of which he has no knowledge.

[9]Text: CSEL 19.278.
[10]Text: CSEL 19.456.

But the just man keeps himself from every sin since he always acts on the knowledge of right and wrong.

Who, then, except the wise man, is able to distinguish the right from the wrong? Hence no fool can ever be just, no wise man unjust. If this is infallible truth, then it is obvious that he is not a fool who refuses to take a plank from a drowning man, or a horse from a wounded man, since it is a sin to act thus, and the wise man does not sin. Even I confess that the truth may *seem* to lie elsewhere, but this would be a mistake derived from our inability to know the real nature of each situation. The solution, then, to this problem derives not from proofs but from definition. Folly is a "wandering from the right path" whether in our actions or words because of our ignorance of the right and the good. Therefore one is not a fool if he does not save himself; he must take care only that he does not harm another, for that is evil. So both reason and truth itself demand.

C. Justice and Virtue:

Lactantius explains justice in its classical definition of "what is due to another." Virtue, which he says is justice, consists in those acts which give to God and to man their due. Worship is due to God; to men, unlimited beneficence:

> VI.10.[11] I have said what is owed to God. I shall say now what must be granted to men, though indeed what you give to man is given to God since man is a likeness of God.
>
> Now the first obligation of justice is to be united in fellowship with men. The first we call "religion" [binding obligation], the second is designated as "mercy" or "feelings of sympathy and kindness towards other human beings." This is the special virtue of the just and of the worshippers of God since in it alone do we find the principle of our common life. For upon animals God did not bestow wisdom, but he made these quite safe from

[11]Text: CSEL 19.514.

danger and attack by means of protection provided by nature. However, since he created man frail and unprotected, with the intent of developing him rather through wisdom, he gave him this disposition towards piety so that people should care for, love, cherish one another, and receive and offer help in the face of every danger. Thus sympathy for one another is the strongest bond among people, and whoever destroys it must be regarded as a wicked murderer. If we are all sprung from the one man God created we are obviously all related. It is therefore the greatest crime to hate a man, even if he harms you. This is why God has commanded us to allow no hostilities to arise, but always to remove them, assuaging enemies by recalling the common bond of nature.

D. Virtue and Immortality:

The power of virtue (and necessarily wisdom) is set forth in a passage of a somewhat dualistic flavor, in which Lactantius affirms that virtue is realized only through evils.

> VII.5[12]... Man is born mortal, but he becomes immortal when he has begun to receive his life from God, that is to follow justice which is found in the worship of God, for God has incited man to look upwards, towards the sky and towards Himself. This happens when one is cleansed in the heavenly bath and lays aside his infancy with all the stain of his former life. Receiving then an augmentation of the divine life-force, he becomes a full and complete person.
>
> Since then God has put before us virtue we may grant that though body and soul are joined together, they are contrary to and fight against one another. The goods of the soul are the evils of the body... and the goods of the body the evils of the soul... For this reason, a just and wise man must live among evils since he thus displays courage, the victor over evils. The unjust man, however, lives among riches, honor, power, for these are goods of

[12]Text: CSEL 19.600.

the body and of the present world. But the unjust live a worldly life nor can they gain immortality because they are devoted to pleasures, which are the enemies of virtue ... God therefore seeks to be worshipped and to be honored as Father, for this reason that man might gain virtue and wisdom which alone bring forth immortality.

E. Eternal Life in the Presence of God:

In spite of the strongly philosophical cast of his work, in his final book, Lactantius describes in strongly apocalyptic language the end of the world and the resurrection of the body. It is in the resurrection that the souls of the virtuous, clothed anew with bodies, will go forever to live with God.

> VII.23[13]. . . They will not have a second birth, for that is impossible, but they will rise again and assume bodies given them by God. They will remember their former life and all their deeds, and dwelling among the celestial goods, they will enjoy the pleasure of inexhaustible riches. They will give thanks to God, now in his very presence, because he has destroyed all evil and raised them up to eternal life and rule.

Our description of Lactantius' philosophical system, however brief, would not be complete without setting forth the image of the Two Ways so central to Book VI. It is an important image because in it Lactantius coalesces an image central to classical philosophy, with an image familiar also in Biblical and early Christian literature; we can see, therefore, with unusual clarity the way in which Lactantius was able both to affirm and to stand in judgment upon the classical tradition. Moreover, the passage carries a rhetorical power which reminds us that in presenting his Christian philosophy Lactantius was not playing intellectual games but directing a persuasive appeal to the pagans. We may note, by the way, that through its eschatological significance the image of the Two Ways here in some measure antici-

[13]Text: CSEL 19.655.

pates the image of the Two Cities which will dominate
Augustine's message a century later.

Cicero shapes the motif of the two ways into a little story
about the hero Hercules, and it may serve to sharpen Lactantius' image if we recall Cicero's story here:

> 1.32[14] When we seek for "the fitting," we must embrace
> all these things with heart and mind. Above all, we must
> determine what sort of person we wish to be and what
> sort of life we wish to live—the most difficult question of
> all. For it is in our youth, when our judgment is weakest,
> that we each determine to follow the kind of life we have
> especially come to love. Accordingly, we are involved in a
> manner and course of life before we can decide what is
> best.
>
> There is a story in Xenophon's work which Prodicus
> tells about Hercules. When Hercules approached adoles-
> cence, the time given by nature for choosing the way of
> life each will enter, he went off to a lonely place, and when
> he saw Two Ways, one of pleasure, the other of virtue, sat
> for a long time considering which of the two was the
> better to follow. Now this, perhaps, could happen to
> Hercules, who was sprung from the seed of Jupiter, but it
> is not likely to happen to us. For we imitate those we
> approve, and are drawn to their pursuits and way of life.
> Frequently, too, we are influenced by the teachings of
> parents and are led to follow their customs and practices.
> Others are carried along by popular opinion, and eagerly
> choose what the majority think best. A few, however, by a
> stroke of good fortune or by the goodness of their nature
> follow the right way of life without parental instruction.

There were, of course, many other versions of this story as
Lactantius' critique witnesses. Lactantius' own version has
been strongly influenced by the Biblical image.

> VI.3.[15] There are two ways, by which human life must
> proceed: the one leads to heaven, the other goes down to

---

[14]Text: Cicero, *De officiis*, LCL .116.
[15]Text: CSEL 19.485.

hell. Poets have introduced this image into their poems, philosophers into their discussions. Philosophers have supposed that the one is the way of virtue, the other of vices. The way of virtue is at first steep and rough, but if anyone overcomes these difficulties and reaches the top, he has henceforth a level road, a bright and pleasant plain, and all the fruits of his labors are rich and pleasant. However, the forbidding aspect of the first stretch frightens some away, and they turn aside and fall into the way of vices. This way at first is lovely, and much more traveled, but a little further on suddenly loses its charm, becomes steep, rough with stones, overspread with thorns, cut deep with the force of raging waters. There you struggle and try to hold your ground, you slip and fall.

The point of the image is clear: it takes the greatest efforts to acquire the virtues, but once acquired, they bring the greatest rewards, and deep and abiding pleasures. Vices, on the other hand, attract us with certain natural allurements and through the illusion of empty pleasures lead us bound to harsh and bitter woes. This would truly be the discussion of a wise man, if philosophers knew the nature and goal of the virtues. But they taught neither what the virtues are nor what reward from God they bring... Therefore, I shall explain how these two ways lead either to heaven or hell. I shall disclose the nature of the virtues which the philosophers did not know, and their rewards, and I shall point out what the vices are and what their punishments...

VI.4. Accordingly, there is one way of virtue and of the good, which leads not as the poets say to the Elysian fields, but to the very citadel of the world, while "the path on the left leads to the punishment of the wicked and sends them to unholy Tartarus" (*Aeneid* 6.542-543). This is the work of that accuser who through false religions turns people aside from the path to heaven and leads them into the way of destruction. This way is designed to present a beautiful prospect, broad and open, delighting the eye with every kind of flower and fruit. Upon this way are placed all the things taken as good on earth: wealth, honor, rest, pleasure, and all alluring charms; but along with these also injustice, cruelty, pride, treachery, lust, passion, hostility, ignorance, falsehood, folly, and the other vices. When one has come to its end whence there is now no return, the road with all its beauty so precipitously stops that one is not able to discover the trickery before he has fallen headlong into a deep abyss. For those who are captivated by the appearance of the present goods, and are busy acquiring and enjoying these, do not foresee what will follow death and so turn from God. Cast into hell, they will be condemned to everlasting punishment.

The way to heaven, however, rises up steep and difficult, savage with bristling thorns and obstructed with jutting rocks. One progresses with much effort and sore feet, and with great care not to fall. Upon this way is placed justice, temperance, patience, faith, chastity, abstinence, fellowship, knowledge, truth, wisdom, and the other virtues; but along with these poverty, shame, struggle, grief and all bitter troubles. Those who stretch forth their hope into the distance and choose the better things will go without the goods of this earth so that they might without encumberment overcome the difficulty of the way. For it is not possible to advance upon or to hold those narrow straits if one surrounds himself with royal magnificence or burdens himself with wealth. Hence we understand that the evil and unjust more easily get what they want since their road slopes down, while the good advance with difficulty toward their desire since they walk on a path which is rough and steep. Because the just man walks upon a harsh and difficult way he must suffer contempt, derision, hatred. For all whom passion and pleasure drag headlong envy those capable of virtue and bear a grudge because someone possesses what they do not. But the just man, poor, humble, despised, subject to outrage, endures all these bitter ills. If he patiently endures the yoke to the last step and end, he will be granted the crown of virtue. God will bestow upon him immortality as a reward for the struggles for justice he endured in life.

These are the ways God has assigned to human life. In each of these he offers good and bad but in reversed order: in the one which has the better order, he has appointed first temporal evils along with eternal goods, in the other, the worse, temporal goods first, and then eternal evils.

A Christian philosophy, then, may be written in the terms familiar to pagans, but it is something quite different from pagan philosophies. It is different because it is, in the first place, not an intimation of the truth, but the truth itself, and it is different, in the second place, because it is not simply a logical system of thought, but a message, a proclamation with a compelling authority, and with the power to change lives. Both Books III and VI contain a sharp critique of pagan philosophy. The following lively address to Cicero is typical of the criticism in Book VI:

VI.11[16] What of Marcus Tullius [Cicero] in his book *On Duties*? Does he also not advise against excessive liberality. His words are: "Liberality, which depends upon one's possessions, drains the very source of kindness. The more you bestow it, the less you are able to bestow it" (2.15.52). A little later he says "What is more foolish than to act in such a way that you are no longer able to do at all what you enjoy doing"(2.15.54). Obviously this professor of wisdom restrains people from human kindness, and urges them to guard carefully their own possessions, to prefer a bank-account to justice. Since he recognized that this was inhuman and wicked, in another chapter, as though repenting, he adds, "Yet sometimes one must give liberally, nor must we reject this kind of liberality. Often we must share our goods with suitable needy people" (2.15.54). Who are "suitable"?

[16]Text: CSEL 19.520.

Those I am sure who are able to pay back and to return thanks!

If Cicero were living now, I should certainly exclaim: "Here, Marcus Tullius, at this very point you have strayed from the path of true justice. You have destroyed it with a single word since you have measured the responsibilities of piety and human sympathy by utility. We ought not give liberally to "suitable" people, but to the "unsuitable.". . . Cast away those shadows and sketches of justice and grasp the true and living image itself. Exercise your liberality upon the blind, the weak, the lame, the forsaken. For unless you give, these must die. They are useless to men, but useful to God who keeps them alive, gives them breath, thinks them worthy of the light.

In an equally rhetorical passage from Book III, Lactantius contrasts the ineffectual words of philosophy with the Word of Truth:

III.26.[17] What therefore they perceived ought to be done since nature demanded it, yet which neither they themselves nor, as they saw, philosophers could do, our heavenly doctrine effects, for it alone is wisdom. Will philosophers who never persuade themselves persuade anyone else? Whose passions will they subdue, whose anger control, whose lust restrain, when they themselves yield to vices and admit that nature is too strong for them? There is new evidence every day to show how powerful the precepts of God can be in human minds, since they are simple and true. Give me a man full of anger, foulmouthed, unbridled. With only a few of the words of God "I shall make him as gentle as a lamb" (Terence, *The Brothers* 4.1.18). Give me one who is grasping, greedy, and avaricious, you shall have him back a generous man bestowing his wealth with open hand. Give me a person fearful of pain and death, and soon he will despise torture, fire, and wild animals. Give me a man

[17]Text: CSEL 19.259.

lustful, lecherous and debauched; soon you will see him sober, chaste, restrained. Give me someone who is cruel and thirsting for blood; soon his madness will be transformed into true mercy. Give me an unjust man, a foolish man, a sinner; forthwith, he will be just, wise, and righteous. All wickedness will be washed away in one bath. So great is the power of the divine wisdom, that once poured into the human heart, it drives out at a single blow folly, the mother of sins. For this, there is no need of money, books or the midnight oil. This is done freely, easily, quickly. Just open your ears, and let your heart thirst for wisdom. Never fear: we are not selling water, we do not offer the sun for a price. The fountain of God, most abundant and overflowing, is available to all; this celestial light arises for all who have eyes to see. Who of the philosophers has ever offered this, or could offer it if he wished? Though they wear away their lives in the study of philosophy they are unable to make anyone else better, or even themselves, if nature offers the slightest obstruction. At its best, their wisdom does not destroy vices; it merely hides them. But the precepts of God so transform the whole man, and from the old renders him so new that you do not recognize him as the same person.

To imply, as Lactanitus does here, that the message of salvation directs its transforming power to the moral life of the individual is not to offer a new theme to Christian apologetic. The theme grew readily enough out of the claim to good living inherent in the primitive Defense, and was not alien to the emphasis upon judgment and the moral consequences of idolatry found in the typical Exhortation. Tertullian in his *Apology*, a classic Defense as we have seen, drew a contrast between the moral weakness of philosophers and the moral strength and innocence of the unlettered Christians to serve as a preface to his concluding vision of the Judgment. But in Lactantius the theme acquires a new power. In the competition between the Christian philosophy and the other philosophies Lactantius scores a major success in the absolutely assured claim of moral transformation, for the problem of ethics lay at the heart of much of ancient philosophy. Moreover, the insistent rhetoric of the repetitive demand to "give me a man, and I will make him new" carries Lactantius' system outside the realm merely of philosophical reflection. The yearning of the speaker, the appeal to the emotions of the audience felt in the rhetoric, belong to exhortation (we may recall the concluding appeal of Clement of Alexandria's *Exhortation*), and are among the factors which turn Lactantius' philosophical system into a Christian message. The transforming power of the message finds enablement through the words of the messenger.

Yet a word of caution is appropriate. We may admire and share Lactantius' enthusiasm for the morally regenerative power of the message of a Christian philosophy, but if the categories—the scheme of virtues and vices—have a fundamentally pagan structure, do we after all have a fully Christian message? Augustine, searching for a philosophy of history, will challenge the very structures of traditional pagan thought.

Augustine, City of God

In Augustine, the historical and political implications of the message find an expression with a richness far surpassing any of the statements of his predecessors. The course of events in Augustine's life had led him to be a figure of considerable political importance by the time he began to write the *City of God*. A brilliant student of rhetoric, he had as a young man of about 30 years won the position of Professor of Rhetoric and Imperial Orator in Milan where the Court was then residing. It was here that he met the bishop Ambrose, under whose tutelage he was converted. Ambrose presented the young Augustine an image of a Bishop almost incessantly involved in the major political events of his day, both advising and threatening the Emperors in the battles between paganism and Christianity which led to the famous edicts of 391 and 392 mentioned above.

Thus when Augustine became Bishop of the relatively small Catholic community of Hippo Regius (near modern Annaba in Algeria), his training and experience, the image of Ambrose, and probably his own inclination as well, urged him to political activity. In his earlier years as Bishop, he sought the support of the Imperial arm to weaken and destroy Donatism, widespread in Africa, and whose adherents in his own episcopal seat of Hippo Regius outnumbered the Catholics. Eventually the Emperor sent a Commissioner, Marcellinus, to effect a settlement of the differences between the Catholics and Donatists, and a judgment was made in 411 decisively in favor of the Catholics. But by 411 Alaric the Goth had already sacked Rome (the pillaging occurred in 410) and pagans had raised the cry that the fall of Rome was the punishment sent by the gods for abandoning their temples. About the same time Volusianus, a distinguished pagan with a Christian mother, a Roman senator and proconsul of North Africa, was in Carthage (in 411-412). He urged Augustine personally by letter (Letter 135) to clear away some of his own doubts, and Marcellinus explained in detail (Letter 136) the difficulties which still deterred his friend Volusianus from becoming a Christian. Among these was the fear that Christian faith could only mean the destruction of the State. Out of this background emerged the *City of God*, a political manifesto based on a radical Christian interpretation of history. Although Augustine originally undertook to silence those who charged Christians with the disasters that had befallen the Empire, over the years the work grew into a major interpretation of Christian faith and its significance for society. Begun in 413, the work was not completed until at least 426 A.D.

It seems clear that Augustine intended the message conveyed by this work to be directed to a virtually universal audience. As we have seen, apologetic literature always assumed that Christians would find the message directed to pagans of benefit to themselves. Augustine specifically addresses the *City of God* to Marcellinus, a Christian:

1.[18] In this work, Marcellinus, my dear son, I am
fulfilling a promise made to you, for I have undertaken to
defend the city of God against those who prefer their own
gods to its Founder. . . It is a great and difficult task, but
God is our helper.

But Marcellinus was intent on the conversion of Volusianus, and, no doubt, of other pagans, too. Augustine's book
is thus an exposition of Faith which Christians could use as
a message to pagans. At the same time, Augustine must have
expected pagans to read the book for themselves. Hence, in
the course of the book Augustine directly addresses sometimes pagans, sometimes Christians.

   The *City of God* may, indeed, be seen as the culmination
of all the efforts which had hitherto been made to bring the
message of Christian faith to the pagans. It is a massive,
sometimes rambling work which finds a focus in the definition and interpretation of the twin conceptions of the Heavenly City and the Earthly City. Within its ample boundaries
Augustine takes time to discuss, often at length, topics of
varied interest: whether Christian virgins raped in the recent
sack of Rome are nevertheless innocent; whether pygmies
are descended from Adam or whether there are men on the
Antipodes; whether miracles still occur, with many contemporary examples given, some personally witnessed. But it
must not escape our notice that within the vast scope, and
through this somewhat conversational method, Augustine
brings to discussion at one time or another virtually all the
topics that have been central to the Christian message to the
pagans as we have seen it developed in its various forms.
One will find, for example, in his pages:

* a critique of pagan gods according to the division of
   gods of the poets, gods of the State, gods of the
   philosophers;
* a narrative of Biblical History;
* a demonstration of the striking coincidence between
   Prophecy and Fulfillment;

[18]Text: CCL 47.1.

* the contrast between Philosophy and the Scriptures;
* statements designed to establish a theodicy;
* proof of the Resurrection and affirmation of the Last Judgment;

The disposition of these topics is determined by Augustine's overriding aim to elucidate the conception of the Two Cities. Christian apologetic had frequently contrasted the communion of saints with the fellowship of demons, had persistently to answer the charge that Christians formed a society aloof from, and cancerous to, Roman society. Augustine recognized that the question of the nature of the two societies lay at the heart of the Christian message. Given his own political inclination, and the political crisis of the time, it was inevitable that he should place this theme at the center of his work. Yet in spite of the fame of his work and the popularity of the image "City of God," there is a widespread ignorance of Augustine's vision. I shall therefore attempt a summary interpretation of the idea of the Two Cities, and then offer selections in which Augustine can speak for himself to define their natures.

Augustine believed that individuals find in like-minded people a fellowship of "loves"—of desires and values—and that societal institutions are the embodiment of these corporate values. Ultimately there are just two contrasting desires which motivate men and women, love of self and love of God. The former expresses itself in a craving for acquisition and a thirst for domination; its characteristic attitude is pride. The latter expresses itself in a chaste use of the goods of the earth directed always towards enabling the growth of love, and in joyful obedience to the will of God; its characteristic attitude is humility. These loves have determined the character of the two societies and their institutions. The society of people motivated by self-love are actually or potentially in a state of civil war, and the peace they offer cannot be a true and just peace. Their city is symbolized by Babel—Confusion. There can in fact be true peace only in the society whose love is God, for peace is the actualization of the order divinely established, and this is effected only in obedience to God. This society is symbolized by Jerusalem—City of Peace.

In practice it is not easy to determine the boundaries of these two societies. Both societies have their origin in the angelic world before creation and time, when the angels destined for beatitude maintained their love in God, but other angels fell away from the love of God. In our own world of men and women, those who turn away from God join the company of the fallen angels in a single society—the Earthly City; while those who give themselves up to obedience to God join the company of the blessed angels and become citizens of the City of God. In this world the two societies are mingled, the members of the City of God living within institutions dominated by the spirit of rebellion, and using them for whatever good they may offer; while sometimes the institutions of grace, such as the church, harbor within themselves, and are used by, those whose love is not fixed on God. Only in the final Judgment will the citizens of the two Cities be completely separated. One point should be emphasized: while the City of God reaches its perfection only in heaven, and while the Heavenly City has a "shadow" in the earthly, historic Jerusalem and in the present church, it is erroneous to assume that Augustine conceives the City of God in the dualistic categories of the temporal and eternal. Rather the City of God is in our present time, and will be forever, a community of angels and redeemed men and women, and it thus transcends the distinction between time and eternity. A broad selection of readings will illuminate this brief sketch.

A. The Term "City of God"

Augustine finds authority for his use of the term in the Holy Scriptures:

> XI.1.[19] We are speaking of the City of God. It finds a witness in that Scripture which, distinguished in its divine authority, surpasses all the literature of all peoples not

[19]Text: CCL 48.321.

through some chance inspiration of those who wrote it, but clearly by the will of a supreme Providence, and thus rises superior to every kind of human talent. Therein it is written: "Glorious things are said of you, city of God" [Ps 87.3], and we read in another Psalm: "Great is the Lord, and exceedingly worthy of praise in the city of our God, in his holy mountain; throughout the entire world his praises extend." A little later in the same Psalm we have: "As we have heard, so have we seen, in the city of the Lord of the mighty powers, in the city of our God; God has established it forever" [Ps 48:1,2,8]. Similarly elsewhere "The stream of the river delights the city of God, the Most High has hallowed his tabernacle; God in its midst shall not be moved" [Ps 46:4,5]. By these and similar witnesses (to list all of which would be tedious), we have learned that there is a certain "City of God," whose citizens we have desired to be, a desire inspired in us by its Founder.

B. The Two Societies Defined: Citizenship

The good and the bad angels are the first denizens of the two cities. The good angels are those who have ever lived in the love of God, the bad those who have fallen away from loving Him. Mankind joins with the angels to form the full estate of those two societies:

> XI.28[20] . . . In this book [Book XI] we shall speak as we are able, and with His help, about the City of God insofar as it does not experience the mortality of this life, but is forever in the heavens. That is, we shall consider the holy angels who clung to God and never did, nor ever shall abandon Him. I have already explained how God originally separated these from those who turned away from the eternal light and became darkness.

> XII.1[21] . . . For surely to cling to God is not a "fault" in a nature which was created with such excellence that though it was indeed capable of change still it should gain

[20] Text: CCL 48.348.
[21] Text: CCL 48.356.

blessedness by clinging to an unchangeable good, that is to God; and that it should not fulfill its greatest longing unless it were blessed, which longing in turn only God could satisfy. For every fault disrupts nature and so is contrary to it. Since it is "natural" to cling to God, to depart from God is a fault. Indeed, by this fault, the real nature is revealed as truly great and praise-worthy.

XII.6[22] The real reason then for the blessedness of the good angels is that they cling to Him who exists in the highest degree. If you seek the reason for the wretchedness of the evil angels, it is because they turned away from Him who supremely is and turned toward themselves who are not Absolute Being. What other name is there for this fault except pride? Indeed, pride is the beginning of every sin. They refused to maintain their strength in relation to Him, and though they would have more "Being" if they would cling to Him who is Absolute Being, they preferred themselves to Him, that is, they preferred what is less.

XII.9[23] We must confess therefore with praise to God that not only is it true of holy men but it can also be said of the holy angels that the love of God has been spread through them by the Holy Spirit given them. And when the Scripture says "It is good for me to cling to God" [Ps 73:28], this "good" applies not only to men, but originally and primarily to the angels. Whoever share this good form, both with Him to whom they cling and among themselves, a holy fellowship; they are one and the same City of God, His living sacrifice, His living temple. I have spoken about the angelic part of that society. I must now speak about that part which is to be joined to the immortal angels, and consists of mortal men, some of whom dwell as strangers in the midst of the changing circumstances of the world, while some have died and rest in the dwelling-places of the departed souls.

[22]Text: CCL 48.359.
[23]Text: CCL 48.364.

C. The Two Societies Defined: History

The two societies are not merely spiritual realities, but insofar as they include mankind, have a temporal history. All the righteous before Christ belong to the City of God, but the earthly city of Jerusalem was a prophetic representation of the perfect City of God.

> XII.28[24]... I must now bring this book (Book XII) to its conclusion. We should, then, suppose that in the first man, Adam, the human race had already sprung up in societies forming, so to speak, two cities. At that time, of course, they could not be recognized, except in the fore-knowledge of God. But from that one man, all people would come, some to join the evil angels in their punishment, some to join the good in their reward administered by the hidden but just judgment of God. For it is written: "All the ways of the Lord are mercy and truth"[Ps 25:10]: his mercy cannot be unjust nor his justice unmerciful.
>
> XV.21[25]... Scripture, then, sets before us the two cities, emerging, as it were, from the common gate of mortality opened in Adam. One is committed to the things of this world, the other to a hope in God, and each will proceed to its just and appropriate end. This is the beginning of history. History will add other generations which will take their origin from Adam, reproducing him, as it were, and condemned therefore with him, like an entire lump of faulty clay rightly discarded. Yet from this clay, God fashions pots, some of which are destined for his reproach and anger, some for his honor and mercy. Upon the former he places the punishment they deserve; upon the latter he bestows the favor they do not deserve. By observing the "vessels of wrath" the heavenly city, which dwells as a stranger on the earth, learns not to place any confidence in the freedom of its own will; its hope lies rather in calling upon the name of the Lord God. For by

[24]Text: CCL 48.385.
[25]Text: CCL 48.487.

nature the will has been made good by a good God, but capable of change, since God, though himself unchangeable, made it from nothing. Accordingly, it is able by its own freedom of choice to fall away from the good and do evil; it is also able to reject the evil and do the good, but only by the help of God.

XV.2.[26] In the history of the world, there has been a sort of shadow, and prophetic sketch of this City, but it has served not so much to exhibit the City as to point to the time in which it was to be revealed. It is called the "holy city" because it was an anticipatory outline of the true "Holy City" that was to appear. The Apostle Paul speaks in Galatians both about that image whose function is to "serve," and about this City which is free. [Augustine quotes here Galatians 4:21-31 where Paul allegorized the relation of Hagar and Sarah: Hagar the servant represented the old covenant, the historical city of Jerusalem; Sarah the free-woman, the new covenant, the Jerusalem above, which is "our mother."] This method of allegorizing, based on Apostolic authority, shows us how we can understand the writings of the two Testaments, Old and New. In some respects, the earthly city has been made to form an outline sketch of the heavenly City. The sketch does not point to itself but to something else whose interests it therefore "serves."

XVIII.47[27]... Not even the Jews, I think, dare argue that no one has belonged to God except the Israelites from the time of Isaac's first descendants after the rejection of Esau. As a people, it is true, they and no other might properly be called the "people of God." But they cannot deny that among other races, too, there have been individuals who belong to the true Israelites, not the Israelites of the earthly society, but those of the heavenly, as citizens of the Fatherland above. For if they deny it, they are easily refuted by the remarkable case of holy Job.

[26]Text: CCL 48.454.
[27]Text: CCL 48.645.

He was neither a native nor a proselyte, that is a resident alien, but was an Idumaean reared in Idumaea, and there he died. The Holy Word praises him so highly that it declares none of his contemporaries his equal in justice and piety [Job 1:8].

D. The Two Societies Defined: Character

Though Augustine describes the character of the Two Societies in various ways, he frequently repeats a few basic contrasts: humility and pride, obedience and domination, peace and disorder, love of God and love of self. And just as Jerusalem is a symbol of the City of God, Babel is the symbol of the City of Man. In a passage recalling a theme central to the Christian message from the time of Paul's Areopagus speech, Augustine locates the source of the confusion in the ignorance of the true God by those who think themselves wise.

XIV.13[28] Holy Scripture teaches that humility is the primary virtue now in the City of God, dwelling as it does a stranger in this world. We also learn that it is the virtue especially commended in Christ, its King, while its opposite, the vice of pride, especially controls his adversary, the devil. Certainly, the great difference between the cities of which we speak is this: the one is a society of godly people, the other of ungodly, each with the angels which belong to it; in the one the love of God is foremost, in the other, love of self.

XIV.28[29] Two loves therefore have formed these two cities. The earthly city has arisen from a love of self which despises God, the heavenly city from a love for God which disregards one's self. The one has its pride in itself, the other glories in the Lord. The one seeks the esteem of men; the other values only this, that God is witness to its conscience. The one raises itself high in its own glory; the other says to God: "You are my glory, you lift up my

[28]Text: CCL 48.435.
[29]Text: CCL 48.451.

head" [Ps 3:3]. In the one, the lust for power controls both the rulers and the ruled; in the other, those with authority and those in their care serve one another in love, the former by good counsel, the latter by willing compliance. The one cultivates its strength in the exercise of its own powers; the other says to God: "I delight in you, O Lord, my strength" [Ps 18:1].

XV.7[30]. . . This is the distinguishing mark of the earthly city, that it worships God or the gods so that it might with their help rule through victories and an imposed peace, not because it has any regard for the welfare of its subjects, but because it has a passion for power. Indeed, the good use the world to enjoy God; the evil, on the other hand, wish to use God to enjoy the world.

XVI.10[31] The generations from Shem must be kept in mind if we are to see the city of God after the flood, just as the generations from Seth revealed it before the flood. This is why, after Holy Scripture had revealed the earthly city in Babylon [Babel], that is in "confusion," it gives an account of the generations from Seth to Abraham. . . . it was from the arrogant pride which built a tower to reach to heaven—a symbol of godless self-exaltation—that the city, which is to say the society, of the godless appeared.

XVI.17[32] At this time there were three distinguished powers among peoples whose "city" belonged to people "born of earth," that is, a society of men living according to men under the power of the fallen angels. Those were the Scythian, Egyptian, and Assyrian, but the Assyrian was much the most powerful, much the proudest. . . The domination of the godless city was greatest, therefore, in Assyria. Its capital was that Babylon whose name was so appropriate to a city of the earth-born. It means "confusion" [Babel].

[30]Text: CCL 48.460.
[31]Text: CCL 48.511.
[32]Text: CCL 48.521.

XVIII.41[33].... Has any people, any senate, any public magistrate of the ungodly city ever attempted to adjudicate among these almost innumerable controversies of the philosophers, approving and accepting some, refuting and rejecting others? Has it not cherished in its bosom without any distinction a confusion of opinions held by men who disagree not about lands, or houses, or financial accounts but about the nature of the good life. If in some cases they spoke the truth, they spoke falsehood also with the same licence, so it is not in vain that such a city has acquired the symbolic name "Babylon." Babylon means confusion, as I said above. It makes no difference to its king, the devil, how torn it is by opposing errors which it maintains alike by its great and manifold ungodliness.

That race, however, that people, that city, that commonwealth, those Israelites who believe the oracles of God, have in no way confused false prophets with the true in equal licence, but have agreed among themselves, and without dissension they have acknowledged and held the authors of the Sacred Scriptures to speak the truth. For such, the authors of Scripture were themselves philosophers, that is, lovers of wisdom, they were themselves the wise, themselves theologians, themselves prophets, themselves teachers of righteousness and piety. Whoever took his wisdom from them and lived according to them, lived and grew wise not according to men but according to God who spoke through them. There, if sacrilege was prohibited, God forbade it; if it was said, "Honor your father and mother" [Ex 20:12] God commanded it; if it was said: "You shall not commit adultery, you shall not kill, you shall not steal [Ex 20:13-15] and such like it was not human tongues but divine oracles which uttered them. Whatever truths philosophers were able to see among their false conjectures, and of which they undertook to convince people by laborious disputation—for example, that God created the world and rules it most

---

[33]Text: CCL 48.637.

providentially, or the integrity of virtue, love of native land, trust in friendship, good works and everything concerned with an upright character—all this they taught without any knowledge of the end or means implied. In the heavenly city these principles were commended to the people by prophetic, that is, divine voices, speaking of course through men. They were not drilled in by dreary argumentation; whoever came to know them was afraid to disregard not the reasonings of a man, but the word of God.

E. The Relationship of the City of God to the City of Man, and to Civil Governments

Though Augustine sees political institutions as capable of being controlled by, and, to that extent, embodying, love of God or love of self, he recognizes the essential neutrality of institutionalism as such, and knows that there are citizens of the City of God living in the society controlled by the citizens of the City of Man, while even the church harbors those who belong to the City of Man. Though an idolatrous society politically organized embodies the City of Man, yet insofar as it establishes peace it fulfills the purposes of the City of God and to that extent Christians respect it and participate in its life.

> 1.35[34]...The City of Christ should remember that among its very enemies lie concealed its future citizens so that it should not think it unprofitable to endure those who are hostile since they may become confessors. Similarly, the City of God harbors wihin itself, as long as it dwells a stranger on earth, those who are united by common participation in the sacraments, but will not share the eternal destiny of the saints. In some cases, these people cannot be discerned; in some cases it is clear who they are. They do not hesitate along with our enemies to blaspheme the God whose sign they bear, sometimes filling the theatres with them, sometimes the churches

[34]Text: CCL 47.33.

with us. Yet one will despair much less of their repentance if among the most outspoken adversaries there lie concealed those destined, however little they know it, to be friends. Certainly in this world the two cities are intertwined and commingled—until they are separated at the Last Judgment.

XVIII.54[35]. . . I have shown as far as I thought proper the historical course of these two cities, the heavenly and the earthly, which are intermingled from the beginning of time to the end. The earthly city has made false gods for itself as it wished, creating them both from historical figures and from other sources, in order to worship them with sacrifices. The heavenly City, which dwells as a stranger on the earth, does not make false gods, but is itself made by the true God whose true sacrifice it becomes. Both alike use temporal goods, both alike suffer misfortunes, but with a different faith, a different hope, a different love, until they are separated at the Last Judgment. Then each will come to its destined end, to which there will be no end.

XIX.17[36] The earthly city, which does not live by faith, strives for an earthly peace and binds the concord of citizens in a relationship of ordering and obeying, so that it arrives at a sort of agreement of human wills on issues concerned with our mortal life. The heavenly city, or rather the part of it which lives by faith and dwells as a stranger in the midst of mortality, must use that peace until the mortality, which necessitates an earthly peace, passes away. While it lives its life of bondage as a stranger within the earthly city (with the promise, however, of freedom in the gift of the Spirit), it does not hesitate to obey the laws of the earthly city, for the laws provide for the ordered maintenance of mortal life, and since mortality is common to all, the two cities should agree on matters pertaining to mortality.

[35]Text: CCL 48.656.
[36]Text: CCL 48.683.

The earthly city, however, had a species of "wise men" of its own (rejected of course by the heavenly learning) who either through their own conjectures or the deception of demons believed that many gods were to be associated with human life... The heavenly City, on the other hand knew that one God alone was to be worshipped, and thought that he must be served only with that service which in Greek is called *latreia* [worship] and is owed to none but God. As a result of this difference, the heavenly City could not share the laws of religion with the earthly city and in this respect had to stand apart from it, a burden to its opponents. It had, therefore, to endure their anger, hatred and persecution, except when it restrained their insolence, sometimes through fear of its growing numbers, always with divine help.

While then this heavenly City dwells a stranger on the earth it calls forth citizens from every tribe and language and binds them together in a pilgrim society. It cares not at all about the differences in those customs, laws, and institutions by which the earthly peace is achieved and maintained. It does not nullify or destroy them, but rather preserves and follows whatever differences among the nations contributed to one and the same end of earthly peace, provided only they offer no obstacle to the religion which teaches that the one highest and true God must be worshipped.

Thus the heavenly City, though dwelling here as a stranger, uses the earthly peace. With due respect to piety and religion, it seeks and guards a harmony of human wills in matters pertaining to the mortal nature of man, and recalls this earthly peace to its heavenly counterpart. For a rational creature, this heavenly peace alone can be regarded as a true peace, for it is a perfectly ordered and perfectly harmonious fellowship of those who enjoy God and one another in God.

F. The City of God the only True Society

All of the definitions of Augustine in this work move ultimately towards a primary goal: to demonstrate against those who find Christian faith destructive to the state that in fact only in the knowledge and love of the one true God is there possible a truly healthy society. Augustine's fundamental message in the *City of God* is precisely that God is the end after which society strives and in obedience to whom society must organize itself. Because the pagans have worshipped false gods their society has never been in the fullest sense of the word, a true society. In discussing this, Augustine draws much of his thought from classical sources, analyzing the definitions Cicero works out in *On the Republic*. His notion of peace, which becomes central to the work, is not much different from the view of justice favored in Plato's *Republic*. Thus the *City of God* is a Christian answer to the centuries of classical pagan efforts to describe the ideal society. The boldness by which Augustine undertakes to give an authoritative Christian answer to the problems of political theory raised by the entire classical tradition could only intensify the force of his message.

> XIX.11[37] We could say, therefore, that peace, like eternal life, is the goal of all that we value. For the City of God, to which we have devoted this lengthy discussion, is addressed in the sacred Psalm: "Praise the Lord, Jerusalem; Zion, praise your God, because he has established your gates; he has blessed your sons in you, he has made your boundaries [i.e. your goal] peace" [Ps 147:12-14]... But if I speak a little longer about this, I shall not, I suppose, bore my readers because peace is the goal of this City of which I am speaking, and peace has a charm which is dear to all.

> XIX.13[38] Accordingly, the peace of the body is the ordered regulation of its parts, the peace of the non-rational soul the ordered quiescence of its desires, the peace of the rational soul the harmonious agreement between thought and action, the peace of body and soul

[37]Text: CCL 48.674.
[38]Text: CCL 48.678.

the ordered life and health of the living whole, the peace between mortal man and God, the ordered obedience in faith under the eternal law, the peace among people, an ordered agreement, the peace of a house, the ordered agreement of ruling and obeying between those who dwell therein, the peace of the heavenly City, the perfectly ordered and perfectly harmonious fellowship of those who enjoy God and one another in God, the peace of all things is the calm that comes from order. Order is the arrangement of things both equal and unequal in their proper place.

XIX.23[39]...Where there is true justice, God commands a city ready to obey according to His grace not to sacrifice to anyone but himself. For this reason, among all people who belong to that state and obey God, the soul faithfully rules the body in a legitimate order, and reason rules the passions. Thus as one person who is just, so an assembly or a population of the just, lives by faith which becomes effective through one's love for God, since we are to love God and our neighbors as ourselves. Where this justice does not exist, there is assuredly no assembly of people "joined together through common rights and shared advantages" [Cicero, *Republic* 1.25.29]. If this definition of a people is true, then there is no "people" where there is not such an assembly; nor is there a commonwealth (since there is no "wealth of the people" [common wealth]) where there is no people.

XIX.24[40]...Since the earthly city does not obey the God who commands not to worship any but himself so that in it the mind cannot properly rule the body or the reason the passions, it is universally true that the city of the ungodly lacks true justice. For however well the mind and the reason may seem to rule the body and the passions, if mind and reason do not serve God as he asks to be served, there is no way they can properly rule the body

[39]Text: CCL 48.695.
[40]Text: CCL 48.696.

and the passions. For what sort of intellect can be master over body and passions when it is ignorant of God nor ruled by him, but perverted by corrupting demons themselves viciously passionate. Accordingly the virtues it thinks it has, by which it rules the body and the passions for the sake of achieving and possessing anything at all except God, are themselves vices rather than virtues.

XIX.27[41] Here in this earthly peace justice is found where God commands and man obeys, the mind commands and the body obeys, reason commands and the passions obey—however reluctantly, whether by subduing or withstanding them; when from God himself we seek both the grace whereby we may do well, and forgiveness wherein we have sinned, and we render thanks for the good we receive.

G. The Two Societies: Their Ends

Because the two societies experience the movement of history, they each have their respective ends beyond this world: eternal happiness with God, eternal punishment with the Devil.

XV.1[42]...I have divided the human race into two kinds, those who live according to men, and those who live according to God. I call these metaphorically "Two Cities," that is, two societies, whose ends are, of the one, to rule forever with God, of the other, to suffer eternal punishment with the devil.

XIX.27[43]...In that final peace which is the goal and end of earthly justice, our nature, made whole by immortality and incorruption, will have no faults, there will be no conflict either within ourselves or among ourselves, and so there will be no need for the mind to rule the passions which will not exist. God will rule man, the mind the body, and the pleasure and joy of obedience will be as

[41]Text: CCL 48.698.
[42]Text: CCL 48.453.
[43]Text: CCL 48.698.

great as our happiness in the life and kingdom we share with God. On the other hand, those who do not belong to the City of God will have only eternal misery. This is called the second death since one cannot say that there the soul lives which is cut off from God nor that the body lives which suffers eternal pain. Hence the second death will be more terrible just because it can never hope for an end in death.

H. Christ in the *City of God*

We have seen that in the written message to the pagans, the place of Christ has held a position of great interest. In some cases, virtually no mention is made of Christ, in others, he is chiefly the Logos, creator of the world and the fulfillment of prophecy. In general, there is an evident reticence to explicate the mystery of the atonement. We cannot leave Augustine's masterpiece without asking how Christ appears in his message.

Augustine's fullest discussion of the meaning of the Incarnation emerges from a consideration of the Neo-Platonist doctrine of the demonic. The Christian message characteristically undertook to expose the demons for what they were—the inspiration behind the idols forcing sacrifices on whose fumes they existed. Augustine links his exposé to a very specific, and clearly favored, audience, the Platonists. For the Platonists had developed a doctrine which in one form as we have already observed, saw demons as helpers in man's effort to ascend to the world of eternal realities but also evil spirits inducing him to fall ever further away from the spiritual world to the disintegrating world of purely physical being. They thus postulated two kinds of demons: the good demons were in one sense "Mediators" of the spiritual world; the bad demons, of the "fallen" world of physical disintegration. Augustine demonstrates that these myths as such cannot hold a shred of truth, but he recognizes in their structure the presentiment of the Christian verity. Hence, in the place of the demons Augustine puts the Christian's Christ who is the true Mediator and therefore the only Way to the Platonist's desire for perfect fulfillment.

Christ is the means by which God is revealed to mankind. Though he receives sacrifices, he himself is the sacrifice, and his religion the only way to God. When Augustine presents Christ as "The Way" to a Platonist audience who relied on the authority of their great teachers Plotinus (205-270 A.D.) and his disciple Porphyry (232-305) his tone becomes evangelical, almost pleading.

> XI.2[44] It is very rare indeed for anyone by sheer intellectual effort to move beyond the consideration and knowledge of the whole creation, corporeal and incorporeal, but capable of change, to the unchangeable substance of God and there to learn from God himself that no one but Himself has made the whole world of nature. For God speaks with man not by any corporeal means, as though He would convey his message to us on sound waves, nor by such spiritual bodies as assume the appearance of physical form, those for example which come to us in dreams... He speaks by means of the truth itself, if anyone is capable of hearing with the intellect, not with the body. For He speaks to that part of man which is best and than which only God himself is better. Since man is properly understood, or at least believed, to have been made according to the image of God, it is this "best-part"—wherein he rises above the "lower parts" he shares with the beasts—by which man most closely approximates the God above him.
>
> But dark and ancient vices have weakened the mind which possess by nature reason and understanding. It is therefore unable to rest in the enjoyment of the unchangeable light; indeed it cannot endure the light at all until, through daily renewal and restoration, it acquires a capacity for such felicity. Hence it had first to be instilled with faith, and cleansed. To facilitate the approach to truth through faith, the truth itself, God the Son of God assumed manhood without loss of his Godhead and established the foundation for that faith. Thus man's God

---

[44]Text: CCL 48.322.

provided a way for man to God through the God man. This is the mediator between man and God, the man Christ Jesus, mediator because man, therefore also Way. For if a way "mediates" between the traveler and his goal, he can hope to arrive at his destination. But if there is no way, or he does not know which way to go, what good is it to know where to go? Now there is only one Way perfectly safe against all deviations—that God and man should be one and the same Person. As God, He is the destination, as man He is the Way.

XI.3. He spoke first through the prophets, then in his own Person, later through the apostles as much as he thought sufficient. Then he prepared what we call the canonical Scriptures which are of most reliable authority and which we believe in matters we ought to know on the evidence of our own senses for they are present to us...Those things, however, which are removed from our senses, we cannot know on our own evidence. For these we seek other witnesses and believe those who we think were present at the events described.

X.19[45]... The deceitful demons arrogantly require sacrifice only because they know that worship is owed to the true God. It is not the fragrance from the roasting flesh, as Porphyry said, and some believe, which they enjoy, but divine honors. There are plenty of fumes everywhere and if they wanted more they could have produced them for themselves. The spirits which arrogantly claim divinity for themselves delight not in the smoke from some body but in the soul of the worshipper whom they deceive, vanquish, then control and so block the Way to the true God. Thus while man sacrifices to something besides God, he cannot offer himself a sacrifice to God.

Now the man Christ Jesus became the true Mediator, made Mediator between God and man, just because he received the form of a servant. Though in the form of

---

[45]Text: CCL 47.294.

God He receives sacrifice with the Father with whom he is one God, yet in the form of a servant He chose to be a sacrifice rather than to receive sacrifice, precisely so that no one would think sacrifice due to any creature. In this way He is both priest and oblation, offering himself. Of this he wanted the sacrifice of the church to be the daily symbol, for the church is his own body and learns to offer itself through him.

X.32[46] This is the religion which offers the Way for all to free the soul, for no one can be free except by this way. This is a sort of "Royal Road" alone leading to a kingdom which does not stumble under the might of temporal grandeur but stands secure in the strength of eternity. Porphyry says towards the end of his first Book on *The Return of the Soul* that no one sect could claim that it offered the Way for all to free the soul, whether a philosophy of the fullest truth, or the Indian way of life, or the Chaldeans, or any other, nor had such a Way come to his attention through his study of history. Here he admits that there indeed is such a Way, though he has not seen it...

What then is this universal Way if not that which has been divinely given, not to any one particular nation, but to all nations together. This Porphyry himself, a man of great ability, does not doubt, for he does not believe that divine Providence could have left the human race without this universal Way to the liberation of the soul. For he does not say the Way does not exist, but rather that this great good, this great help was not yet known. And no wonder. For Porphyry lived at a time when the universal Way to free the soul, which is none other than the Christian religion, was opposed by the worshippers of idols and demons and by the rulers of the world...

This then is the universal Way to the freedom of the soul, that is, a way granted by the Divine mercy to all people. No one then who has come to know of it, or will

[46]Text: CCL 47.309.

come to know of it should ask of it: why just now? or why so late? since the human imagination cannot penetrate the mind of Him who provided it. . .

This then is the Way open to all to free the soul. This the holy angels and prophets preached first among a few people who discerned the grace of God as they were able. For the Hebrew race above all — whose commonwealth was a sort of sacred symbol representing and predicting the City of God which was to be gathered from all peoples — for this race the prophets pointed to the Way in tabernacle and temple, in priesthood and sacrifice, sometimes in words transparent in meaning, more often enigmatic and profound. But the Mediator himself, present in the flesh, and his blessed Apostles, revealed the grace of the New Covenant and now quite openly declared what was obscurely signified in former times. . .

This Way purifies the whole person and makes the mortal ready for immortality in his entire being. For the Purifier and Savior, most true, most powerful, took upon himself the whole man for this reason that we should not seek one type of cleansing for what Porphyry calls the intellectual part of man, another for what he calls the spiritual, yet another for the body itself. Apart from this Way which. . . has always been available to mankind, no one has been free, no one is free, no one will be free.

In offering the selections above, I have tried to trace, as fully as possible within a brief space, the contour of Augustine's portrait of the Two Cities. While, as I have shown, the traditional themes of apologetic woven throughout the work stamp the *City of God* with the character of a message to the pagans, we may still ask in what ways the portrait itself of the Two Cities might be expected to speak to pagans. Here, as in the case of Lactantius' Two Ways, we should not be insensitive to the "rhetoric" of the portrait. Augustine paints the Two Cities in deeply contrasting colors and tones. All the pride of human civilization, all the grandeur of Rome, are set in a sinister light, are painted in dark tones, while a bright light constantly bathes the City of God.

By this means, the portrait itself invites decision. At the same time, the portrait carries answers to some of the age-old fears of the pagans, and above all to the fear that Christianity is destructive to the State. Augustine forces the question on to an entirely new plane of discussion by his doctrine of the two loves: the societies of this world carry in their self-love the seeds of their own destruction; it is only in the heavenly society, whose love is centered on God, that men and women can find security and can grow in an unending life. The simplistic retorts of Tertullian to Scapula or of Cyprian to Demetrianus are transformed here into a powerful vision of the infinite potential for the fulfillment of men and women in society. Finally, it is evident that some touches within the portrait have a special appeal of their own, and of none is this more true than the identification of Christ as the Mediator, His religion as the "Royal Road" to freedom.

Augustine, Letters:
Augustine the Bishop and the Conversion of Pagans

Throughout these past three chapters, our study of the message to the pagans has been based on more or less artistic documents designed for a circulation in some measure broad and general. But it will not be inappropriate to follow our discussion of the *City of God* with evidence from the Letters of Augustine for the way in which a distinguished bishop in the fifth century might take advantage of immediate social and political situations to address a message to a very specific pagan audience. Augustine's response to two highly contrasting situations may be taken as representative.

In the first, Augustine had occasion to write to the people of Madaura, a small town which must have been of great personal interest to him since it was only a few miles distant from his birthplace Tagaste, and had provided his elementary schooling. It is difficult to reconstruct with precision what evoked his letter to the people of Madaura. He tells us only that a certain Florentinus came to Hippo to seek his support in a moment of bereavement, supported by a letter from the citizens of Madaura. The letter, he avers, was not in fact necessary, since Florentinus had relatives in Hippo to help him; Augustine suggests therefore that the letter came providentially to offer him an opportunity to present in reply the message to the Madaurans. Augustine's letter is interesting both for the content of the message, and for the dynamics of personal appeal.

Perhaps nothing is so striking as the solidly traditional content of Augustine's message. Written possibly after 400 A.D., the letter strikes themes familiar already in the second century, and having roots, as we have seen, in the earliest Apostolic preaching. At an early point he speaks of the persuasive authority of prophecy and its fulfillment. It is to be noted how very contemporary are the events in which he sees the divine action:

> 232.3[47] The Scriptures have not been silent...about all those historical events our ancestors recorded and passed on to us, nor about the events of our own day...On the contrary, all things come to pass as they were predicted. You see, for example, the Jews torn from their homeland and scattered over almost the entire earth. You see the Word and Law of God going forth from the Jews through Christ to gain and hold the faith of all peoples...You see many sundered from the roots of the Christian fellowship through heresies and schisms...You see the temples of the idols falling into disrepair, destroyed, closed, and transformed to other uses...All this the sacred Scriptures, available now to everyone, long ago affirmed would happen.

Augustine goes on to speak, in the philosophically allusive terms so characteristic of even the earliest apologetic, of God as Creator, and His Word by whom God is revealed:

[47]Text: CSEL 57.513.

232.5 There is a Being which cannot be seen, though creator and originator of all we see, supreme, eternal, unchangeable, unutterable except insofar as it speaks to itself. There is a Being by which that highest majesty speaks and declares itself. This is the Word. The Word shares equality with the One who speaks and brings it forth, and it reveals the One who begets it.

Typically, one finds here also the identification of the Word with Christ, demonstrated to be the Word through His mighty deeds. Augustine, however, makes this traditional motif very much his own by setting it in the perspective of a conception central to his theological understanding—the contrast between pride and humility, the former the essence of human disobedience to God, the latter the distinctive mark of the Christian. We have seen the contrast assume a pivotal position in the *City of God.*

232.6[48] We had first to be brought down from the false arrogance of a towering pride to humility so that we might rise from thence to acquire a true greatness. No way could have been found at once so lofty and so alluring to subdue our rebellious spirit by persuasion rather than force, had not that Word—through which God the Father discloses himself to the angels, which is his Power and his Wisdom, and which the human heart could never have seen, blinded as it is by its passion for things that can be seen—been pleased to reveal himself in a man. Thus he provided for us an example that we should not seek to achieve glory through human pride but rather through divine humility. Accordingly, Christ was not honored with worldly power, he was not rich with worldly wealth, nor was he conspicuous in worldly success. But Christ was crucified, and now is preached throughout the whole earth. What nations in their pride formerly mocked, now only a few individuals mock; what before only a few believed, now entire peoples believe. Formerly only a few arrived at faith, most continued to

[48]Text: CSEL 57.515.

deride when Christ crucified was preached, when the
lame walked, the dumb spoke, the deaf heard, the blind
saw, the dead arose. At length worldly pride has taken
note that nothing on earth is more powerful than the
divine humility. In this way—by the strength of the divine
model—that humility of men and women, so wonderfully
wholesome, guards against the pride which assaults it.

Augustine's final appeal, like that of Paul on the Areopagus, is to the coming Judgment.

> 232.7[49] . . . Fear Him whom the proud world formerly
> mocked and condemned, but now, vanquished, awaits as
> judge. I have expressed as best I could through this letter
> the token of my affection for you. It will be a witness
> against you in the last Judgment when Christ shall establish those who believe in Him, but put to confusion those
> who disbelieve.

We must note yet that in presenting this message to the
people of Madaura Augustine takes advantage of the personal relationship between himself and them. It is a relationship of great respect, even love. He recognizes their deep
feeling for him in the salutation of their letter, for they
addressed their letter "To Father Augustine, eternal salvation in the Lord." Augustine boldly describes how his hopes
were dashed in reading the letter, obviously calculating
carefully the winning psychological effect such an admission will have on his readers. He even suggests that their
expressions of love will be understood as an insult—unless
they accept the message:

> 232.2[50] When I read the salutation of your letter: "To
> Father Augustine, eternal salvation in the Lord," I was
> suddenly animated by a great hope to believe either that
> you had been converted to the Lord and to his eternal
> salvation, or that you wished to be converted by my
> ministry. But as I read further, my heart was chilled.

[49]Text: CSEL 57.517.
[50]Text: CSEL 57.511.

Nevertheless I asked the bearer of the letter whether you were now, or wished to be, Christians. When I learned from his response that nothing was changed, I was deeply grieved that the name of Christ to which you now see the whole world subject, not only has been rejected by you; you even think you should address in mockery myself who claim it.

It is a specially fine touch that in his concluding appeal Augustine returns the affection, and the compliment he has refused to accept, by addressing the citizens of Madaura as his "parents," recognizing by this term the debt he owes to them for providing him with his boyhood education:

> 232.7[51] Arouse yourselves then at last, citizens of Madaura, my brothers, or rather my parents. God has given me this opportunity to write to you.

In our second example, the opportunity to present the message grew out of a much more intense political situation. In the city of Calama, not far from Hippo, in direct disregard of numerous laws (most recently that of the Emperor Honorius in 407) forbidding the public celebration of heathen festivities, pagans had not only held a festival, but also attacked a Christian church, stoning it and endeavoring to set it on fire. A priest was killed, though the bishop (Possidius) whom they also sought to kill, escaped. The citizens, recognizing their crime, summoned Augustine for counsel, and Augustine addressed them in a public assembly. Shortly afterwards, a leading citizen of Calama, Nectarius, addressed a letter to Augustine begging him to encourage a policy of leniency (Letter 90). Augustine's reply (Letter 91) affirms Christian mercy but it also affirms the necessity of punishment as a mode of correction. He proposes therefore that capital punishment be avoided, but that fines be imposed, not so heavy as to destroy the means of livelihood, but heavy enough that there would be no possibility of pagan luxury, and therefore no means of carrying on idola-

[51]Text: CSEL 57.516.

trous festivities. Meanwhile, Possidius went to Rome to lodge a complaint (Letter 95). Eight months later, the trials of the guilty still pending, Augustine received from Nectarius a response to his letter. Nectarius (Letter 103) appealed once more for mercy, in a tone which Augustine regarded as bordering on flippant, but he was clearly eager to build bridges between Augustine and the pagan community. He flatters Augustine for being one whom he could regard as a distinguished philosopher, reaffirms his own patriotism, and declares that he was indeed eager for the City of God which Augustine had in his previous letter urged him to seek, but that it could be found by various ways. Augustine's final letter (104) on this matter reviews once more the case, justifies his earlier opinion, and attempts to answer Nectarius' philosophic ruminations. The situation offered Augustine an opportunity to present the message of the gospel to two audiences and in various ways.

In the first place, we should note how Augustine used the opportunity afforded him by the request of the citizens of Calama for counsel. He does not tell us the content of the message he gave on that occasion, but he hints at how he used what must have been psychologically a most advantageous moment to present the message. One cannot deny an element almost of blackmail, for the suggestion is clear that punishment might be forgiven, at least lightened, for those who become Christians:

> 91.10[52] When I went to Calama recently both to comfort those in distress from such serious trouble and to calm those who were angry, I spoke to the Christians as best I could about what I judged the proper course of action at that time. Then I received the pagans, too, the source and cause of the disaster, since they had asked to see me. I took the opportunity to admonish them about what they should do, if they were wise, not only to free themselves from their present predicament, but to seek their eternal welfare. I, for my part, spoke to them at

[52]Text: CSEL 34.434.

length, and they, for theirs, sought many favors from me.
Still, God forbid that I should be the kind of servant who
likes to entertain requests from those who do not seek our
Lord.

We may well feel that Augustine here took an unfair
advantage of a delicate situation, though his words suggest
that his message went largely unheeded. Yet with these
pagans he does stop short of compulsion. He clearly hopes
that correction might result in their conversion. But more
particularly, he wishes to deprive them of the means of
carrying on idolatrous practices, and to set forth an example
which will discourage any further actions directed against
the Christians. He leaves to God the possibility of a correction which will indubitably result in their conversion. He
reviews the alternatives:

> 104.11[53]... Accordingly, only God knows what time
> will bring, what opportunities or problems we shall meet,
> what changes of heart may arise from the amendment of,
> or hope in, their present circumstances. We cannot tell
> whether God is so angry at this deed that he will grant
> them as a more terrible punishment the very impunity
> they seek; or whether he will judge that some gentle
> compulsion should be brought to bear, as I should like; or
> whether by some punishment harsher but more whole-
> some he will avert the fearful things prepared for them
> through their true conversion to the mercy not of men but
> of God, and so turn their fear to joy.

The message then is presented to pagans without, strictly
speaking, coercion. With schismatics Augustine was less
gentle. In his long struggle with Donatists he eventually
came to feel that it was a Christian obligation to compel
separated brethren to return to the fold.

In the second place, the correspondence with Nectarius
offered an ideal opportunity for Augustine to present the
message to an influential citizen in a context which made

[53]Text: CSEL 34.589.

him especially vulnerable to Augustine's overtures. Again, Augustine took advantage of the situation. In his first letter to Augustine, Nectarius, it is clear, had posed as a patriot, placing himself in the classical tradition of those who deserved well because they had served their country well, and claiming that as an old man in the shadow of death, he wished to leave his country flourishing. Accordingly Augustine challenges him precisely on this point in the opening portion of his reply:

> 91.1[54] I am not surprised that as your body grows chill with old age, your soul burns with the love of your native land, and I praise you for this. I am not reluctant, but happy to learn that not only do you yourself accurately remember, but by your way of life demonstrate that for good men there is no measure or end of caring for one's fatherland. This is why I covet you as a citizen of that heavenly fatherland, for the love of which in my own modest way I undergo labors and dangers on behalf of those whom I should like to see make that fatherland their own. For then you would think there is no measure or end of caring for the small part of it which dwells here as a stranger on the earth. You would be better precisely because you preferred the duties owed to a better state. In its eternal peace you would establish no limit in time to your labors on her behalf...
>
> Consider for a little while those books *On the Republic* from which you have absorbed that deep feeling of a fond citizen that for good men there should be neither measure nor end of caring for the fatherland. Consider, I beg you, and see with what high praises frugality and self-control are there advocated, as well as faithfulness in marriage, and chaste, noble and praiseworthy morals, through which the state grows strong and must therefore be said truly to flourish. But these are the very patterns of behavior which are taught and learned in the churches growing rapidly now throughout the world, so that one might say

[54]Text: CSEL 34.427.

these comprise the instruction given in the "schools of nations." Here above all is instruction in piety whereby the God who is both true and truthful is worshipped. And all those virtues by which the human soul is prepared and made ready to dwell in an eternal and celestial city in a divine fellowship, he not only commands us to attempt, but grants us to possess them...

Take away then all those empty mindless rites of false religion; let people everywhere turn to the true worship of God, to pure and upright morals. There you will see your native land flourishing not through the speculation of fools but through the truth of the wise. Then this native land of your physical birth will be a portion of that fatherland, to which we are born not physically but through faith, where all the faithful saints of God shall flourish after the wintry labors of this life in an unending eternity.

In his second letter Augustine turns Nectarius' claim of love for his country into a direct invitation to become a Christian:

104.10[55]...If you loved your fellow citizens in the grace of God rather than in the manner of worldly men, you would reply to me sincerely that when I urged you to the worship and religion of the most excellent God you gladly heard, and not only would you desire this for them, but would lead the way there yourself. And so the whole affair of your request would end in a great and wholesome joy. Thus through the true and devoted love of that native land which brought you into this world, you would deservedly gain that heavenly fatherland of which you said you had gladly learned when I urged its consideration upon you. Then you would truly be caring for your fellow-citizens, not merely that they might have an empty joy for a time, nor escape a terrible punishment for their crime, but that they might enjoy the grace of eternal happiness.

[55]Text: CSEL 34.589.

Having progressed so far, Augustine will not let Nectarius go without pointing him to "The Way." Here he can proceed from the words of Nectarius who had said that all religions aspire to the heavenly City. But we do not wish merely to aspire, rejoins Augustine; we wish to attain. It is true that Holy Scripture speaks of "Ways," but they are all comprehended in the one Way—Christ.

> 104.12[56]...In the Holy Scriptures we read of both "Ways" and a "Way": "Ways" for example in: "I shall teach the unrighteous your ways, and the ungodly shall turn to you"[Ps 51:13]; "Way" in: "Lead me in your way, and I shall walk in your truth"[Ps 86:11]. These are not distinct, but all are one. About these Scripture says elsewhere: "All the ways of the Lord are mercy and truth"[Ps 25:10]. If one considers these carefully, they give rise to copious discourse and to a most delightful understanding. This I can offer at another time.
>
> 13. Now, however,—for I think I have said enough in my reply to your Excellency—since Christ said "I am the Way"[Jn 14:6], mercy and truth must be sought in him. If we seek these elsewhere, we go astray, following a path that seeks but does not lead to the goal.

One can discover the deft arrangement by which Augustine unfolds his message and appeals to Nectarius only by reading the full text of the letter. But there can be little doubt that the message gained force by attaching itself—and by limiting itself—to those aspects which had a direct and powerful relevance to the perception a leading citizen had allowed himself of his role in society.

[56]Text: CSEL 34.591.

Suggestions for Further Reading

Brown, Peter R.L., *Augustine of Hippo. A Biography*, Berkeley 1967.

Chapters 26 and 27 reveal the way in which Augustine's life and the events of his day helped to shape the *City of God*.

von Campenhausen, H., *The Fathers of the Latin Church*, Trans. M. Hoffman Stanford 1969.

Chapter 3 sets the writings of Lactantius in the context of his life.

Gilson, Étienne, *The Christian Philosophy of St. Augustine*, Trans. L. E. M. Lynch, New York 1960.

Chapter 4, Part II, analyzes the relation in Augustine's thought between the wills and loves of individuals and the existence of the earthly and heavenly societies.

Markus, Robert A., *Saeculum: History and Society in the Theology of St. Augustine*, Cambridge 1970.

A provocative study of Augustine's political philosophy. Markus argues that it was Augustine who "secularized" political institutions.

Norris, Charles N., *Christianity and Classical Culture*, Oxford 1944.

Chapter 5 is a sharp critique of Lactantius' pretentions to a genuinely Christian philosophy; Chapter 12 an appreciation of Augustine's philosophy of history.

Chapter Six

THE MESSAGE TO
THE LEARNERS

From a very early period in church history, instruction in the Christian faith was required of those who sought baptism. This instruction became increasingly formalized until by the third century a well-developed catechumenate had taken shape. As a period of intensive preparation for assuming the rights and responsibilities of professing the name of Christ, the catechumenate offered the opportunity not only to present but to expound with care the Christian message.

Although it is not possible to trace accurately the process of development of the catechumenate from its primitive to its fully developed style, we are able to acquire a fairly clear picture of it in the fourth and early fifth centuries from the *Catechetical Lectures* of Cyril of Jerusalem who was consecrated bishop in 349, and from the writings of Augustine. Cyril delivered, probably in 348 or 349, a series of lectures to advanced Catechumens (properly called the "*photizomenoi*" or "*illuminandi*"—those to be given the light) which afford us an insight into both the content of the instruction and the manner in which the instruction proceeded. From Augustine's pen we have not only sermons on the Creed and on the Lord's Prayer delivered to the Catechumens (the *illuminandi*) in the final stages of their preparation, but an essay *On Catechizing the Uninstructed* in which he responds to an "Instructor" (Deogratias) who asks how he should expound the message in an appealing way to those in the early stage of the catechumenate. (Recent doubts that the treatise was actually directed to the issue of catechetical instruction have not generally dislodged the traditional view of its purpose.) Of special importance also are the sermons of John Chrysostom (ca. 347-407) preached to the *photizomenoi* and neophytes at Antioch. Much earlier Tertullian who might well have been himself a catechist, wrote a treatise to candidates for baptism which undoubtedly reflected his own perspective on the message appropriate to the Catechands. Occasional references to the instruction appear, as a matter of course, in other patristic writings as well, while a good account of its form in the early third century is given in Hippolytus' *Apostolic Tradition.*

Origen, Against Celsus

By the third century at least, the catechetical instruction was divided into several stages. In his *Against Celsus* Origen speaks of an initial stage, undertaken by private individuals, followed by a more advanced stage. Contrasting the instruction in the pagan schools with that of the Christian he says:

> 111.51[1] Philosophers who discourse in public do not select their hearers, but whoever wishes stands and listens. Christians, however, as far as possible carefully scrutinize the lives of those who wish to hear them. Then they instruct them privately, and the learners do not come to the assembly until they seem to have made sufficient progress in their determination to live properly. At that time they introduce them, forming a class of beginners just admitted who have not yet received the token of cleansing, and another of those who demonstrate to the best of their ability their choice to desire only what is appropriate to Christians. Among the Christians some

[1] Text: SC 136.120.

have the responsibility to make careful inquiry into the
lives and morals of those who come to them, for they
wish, on the one hand to prevent infamous characters
from entering their assembly, but on the other to receive
wholeheartedly those they can daily improve.

Our sources suggest that the initial stage of the catechumenate (the catechumenate proper) lasted for two or three
years during which time the sincerity of the individual seeking instruction was tested. This was followed by a period of
more intense instruction during Lent. It is during this latter
period that the first eighteen of Cyril's lectures on a version
of the Nicene Creed were delivered. But following the principle, as already suggested by Origen, that the deepest mysteries of the faith, the most profound aspects of the message,
should not be delivered. to minds not ready, Cyril concluded his instruction in a further stage, a series of lectures
during the week after Easter, in which he expounded the
meaning of the initiatory rites the candidates had undergone
on Easter Eve. It is not important to the present consideration that some scholars have attributed these "Mystagogic
lectures" not to Cyril but to his successor, John. In either
case, they represent a final stage of instruction.

Although the examples we have of this catechetical
instruction are most striking perhaps for their individuality,
implying considerable freedom on the part of the instructor
for shaping the message as he wished, nevertheless there are
some noteworthy constants in the content. It seems clear in
the first place that catechumens would be expected to
acquire a knowledge of the Bible, of the Creed, and of the
Lord's Prayer. Second, at its best, instruction in this knowledge offered exposition of the nature of Saving History, and
definitions of the meaning of Christian language about God
and Christ, and man and his world. At the very least, it
seems to have insisted on the necessary distinctions in the
way Catholics and heretics understood the Bible and the
doctrine of the creeds. In any case, of all the doctrines none
found in the catechetical instruction a better opportunity
for vivid presentation than that of the Resurrection of the

Dead and the Last Judgment. Third, catechetical instruction was invariably concerned to present Christian faith not merely as a creed to be understood, but as a style of life to be lived. This sometimes led in the fourth place to a special emphasis upon the significance of the Holy Spirit, who was to be received in the baptismal rites, and through whom lives were to be reformed and fashioned for a new mode of behavior.

Augustine, On Catechizing the Uninstructed

Augustine's treatise *On Catechizing the Uninstructed* presupposes, as we have seen, instruction at the early stage of the catechumenate, when the learners are technically called "hearers" and before they have been formally accepted as candidates for baptism. Augustine, at Deogratias' request concerns himself both with the message and the manner appropriate to this early stage. The content of the message at this point is the story of God's acts as recorded in the Bible. The content may be expounded in longer or shorter form. He describes the longer form thus:

> 111.5[2] It is a full account whenever the catechist begins from the words "In the beginning God created the heaven and the earth" [Gen 1:1] and continues to modern times in the life of the church. Yet we ought not to recite from memory, even if we are able to do so, the whole of the Pentateuch, and all the books of Judges, Kings and Ezra, as well as the Gospels and the Book of Acts, nor should we describe and expound in our account everything contained in these books. There is neither time nor any need for this. Rather, you should present everything in summary form and with perspective, selecting the more wonderful events which are pleasant to hear and belong to the turning points of history, events of such importance that it would be quite wrong to pass on after a

[2]Text: CCL 46.124.

> superficial glance at them. One must pause over them as
> though to unravel and explore and to present them to the
> minds of the learners for both scrutiny and wonder. The
> rest can be introduced in a rapid survey. By this principle
> of subordination, what we especially wish to emphasize
> stands out more sharply, while we shall not weary the
> person whose interest we wish to arouse, nor confuse him
> with facts when our intent is to instruct.

Augustine concerns himself with the best manner of presenting the message to learners, in part, at least, because
Deogratias was worried that his instruction was intolerably
dry. Hence we see here that for Augustine a basic principle
of good teaching is selectivity. But it is important to note
that he asks for selectivity not only to afford clarity of
perspective to the learner, but apparently also for a sound
theological reason, that is, to draw attention to the fact that
we perceive God's saving acts at critical moments in history,
rather than in the warp and woof of daily events which make
up the fabric of human life.

Augustine proceeds to a second principle of sound peda-
gogy, that of relevance. He insists on relevance of the most
dynamic sort, the kind of relevance that brings the learner
into a personal encounter with Christ, who is, after all the
heart of the message:

> IV.8[3] Christ came for this reason above all, that man
> might learn how much God loves him. This he was to
> learn so that a love towards the God who first loved him
> might be kindled in his heart, and he would love his
> neighbor not only because God demanded it but because
> God Himself became a neighbor by loving man who was
> not merely not His neighbor but indeed a distant
> stranger. Everything in Sacred Scripture written before
> Christ was written to announce the coming of the Lord.
> Whatever afterwards was entrusted to literature and
> established by divine authority speaks of Christ and
> counsels love. It is clear then that not only do the Law and

[3] Text: CCL 46.128.

the Prophets—which, when the Lord spoke, alone constituted Holy Scripture—hang on these two commandments of love to God and love to neighbor, but likewise whatever other books of sacred literature were later written for our salvation and handed down to memory...

Now nothing is more opposed to love than envy, and pride is the mother of envy. Therefore, the same Lord Jesus Christ, the God-man, is both a token of the divine love towards us, and an example for us of humility in man, so that our swelling pride might be cured by a counteracting medicine stronger than the disease. Proud man represents a profound misfortune, but a humble God even deeper pity. Since this love, then, is the end to which you should direct everything you say, tell the story in such a way that the learner will by hearing believe, by believing hope, and by hoping love.

Augustine recognizes that there are many reasons which bring people to desire to hear the message. Some merely wish to please friends, or to escape the displeasure of enemies. These should not be rejected, for they may eventually be led to undertake instruction for better reasons. But a person is most ready for instruction when he comes with some sense of fear, the result perhaps of divine warning. Even so, the catechist's first task is to turn away his mind from signs and wonders and direct the heart to love:

VI.10[4] But if by chance he says he has been warned or frightened by some divine sign to become a Christian, he offers us a most wonderful opportunity to begin by showing God's great care for us... One can then point out that the Lord would not be warning or urging him to become a Christian through such signs had he not wished him to make his way more securely...along the path already prepared in Holy Scripture. Then beginning, as I said, with the fact that God made everything very good you may continue to modern times. Only remember, that we

[4]Text: CCL 46.130.

must explain those events we narrate in such a way that
we direct everything to that goal of love, from which,
whatever is said or done, we must never turn aside our
gaze.

Finally, Augustine stresses the importance of the doctrine
of the Resurrection and Judgment, not merely as a necessary dogma of belief, but as an incentive to Christian behavior. He also asks the catechist to recognize that Christian
behavior is not unrelated to orthodox doctrine, and hence
to warn the catechand against all unbelief and heresy.

VII.11.[5] When the narrative of Saving History has
been completed, then you must speak of the hope of the
resurrection. Keeping in mind the capacity and ability of
the learner and the amount of time itself, you must,
against the vain derision of unbelievers, consider the
resurrection of the body, the goodness of the Last Judgment for the good, its severity for the evil, its reality for
all. You should recount the penalties of the ungodly with
loathing and dread, but describe with longing the kingdom of the just and the faithful, the heavenly city, and its
joy.

Then one must prepare the learner for and alert him to
human weakness in the face of the trials and the stumbling blocks he will meet both within and without the
church—outside the church in the persons of pagans,
Jews, or heretics; within the church in the "straw" of the
Lord's "threshing-floor." You do not need to answer
every possible question such people raise, or refute all
their depraved views. Without taking much time, simply
point out that such stumbling blocks have been predicted, and show the value of temptations for the discipline of the faithful and the antidote to temptations in the
example of the patience of God who has determined to
allow them to persist to the end.

While you are preparing the learners for those con-

[5]Text: CCL 46.131.

fused multitudes whose bodies fill the churches, you
should mention briefly and appropriately the precepts of
honorable Christian behavior. Warn them not to be led
astray by drunkards, or by the avaricious, or by cheats,
gamblers, adulterers, fornicators, lovers of the shows,
magicians, enchanters, astrologers, or soothsayers of
whatever kind. They should not be seduced by such
people into thinking that they will not suffer punishment
just because they see many so-called Christians loving
evils of this sort, participating in them, defending them,
even exhorting and persuading others to continue in this
kind of life, and tell them that the church must endure
such people within it until their separation at the end of
time.

For Augustine, then, the first stage of the catechumenate
should convey a message whose themes were a traditional
part of Christian apologetic, especially the saving acts of
God revealed in Biblical history, prophecy and fulfillment,
and the resurrection and the Judgment. We note, however, a
significant difference in the way Christ is to be presented: he
is not only the Logos, or the fulfillment of prophecy, or even
merely Savior; he is to be seen ultimately as a Person to be
loved.

Cyril of Jerusalem, Catechetical Lectures

The lectures of Cyril of Jerusalem take us to a more
advanced stage of instruction. The learners have been
approved as candidates for baptism, and Cyril uses the
creed as the framework for the message he wishes them to
hear during the Lent preceding their baptism. It is impossible in the space available here adequately to excerpt or even
summarize these great lectures (with the Mystagogic lectures delivered during Easter week, they comprise two
volumes [61 and 64] in the "Fathers of the Church" series). I
shall therefore focus on two aspects of his teaching which
are perhaps the most interesting—and relevant—to us.

First, because Cyril was writing in a period when the

church was in great turmoil over the definition of orthodoxy, particularly in relation to the doctrine of the Trinity,
his lectures reflect his concern that the learners distinguish
between the true message of the Catholic church and the
false message of heretics. Although he is careful everywhere
to distinguish between what he regards as Catholic belief on
the one hand and heresy on the other, it is in his discussion
of the Church that he gives to the learners a particularly
strong exhortation to remain within the Catholic church.

> 18.26[6] The term "ecclesia" is used of different things. It
> has been used of the crowd in the theatre at Ephesus:
> "Saying this, he dismissed the crowd" [Acts 19:40]. One
> might properly and truthfully speak of the *ecclesia*, or
> assembly, of the wicked, that is, the confederacies of the
> heretics—Marcionites, Manichaeans, and the rest. The
> faith securely handed down to you now speaks of "one
> holy Catholic Church" (*ecclesia*), precisely for this pur-
> pose, that you might flee from those abominable confed-
> eracies, and remain always in the holy Catholic Church in
> which you were born again. So whenever you go to a new
> city, do not ask simply, "Where is the church" [i.e. the
> building], for the ungodly heretics like to call their chap-
> els "churches," too; nor where is the church [i.e. the
> assembly], but where is the *Catholic* church. This is the
> term which identifies it as holy and the mother of us all.
> She is the bride of our Lord Jesus Christ, the only begot-
> ten Son of God. For it is written: "As Christ loved the
> church and gave himself for it," etc. [Eph 5:25], and it is
> the type and likeness of "the heavenly Jerusalem, which is
> free and the mother of us all" [Gal 4:26]. Formerly she
> was barren, but now is the mother of many children. . . If
> we have been taught within this holy Catholic Church,
> and within her live virtuously, we shall have the kingdom
> of heaven and inherit eternal life.

The second aspect of Cyril's message which we should
note is his eloquent and emphatic teaching on the Holy

[6]Text: PG 33.1048.

Spirit, a theme obviously appropriate to candidates for baptism. Two lectures (16 and 17) are devoted to the teaching. Unfortunately, the text at this point is not secure. There is evidence of some interpolation at an early point in Lecture 16 and some scholars have disputed whether all the teaching represented in these two lectures is consistent with what we know of Cyril. But apart from the interpolation just mentioned, the scholarly consensus continues to accept the lectures as genuinely Cyril's, and we may proceed on that assumption.

At the very beginning of his series of lectures, Cyril had alluded to the central place occupied by the Holy Spirit in the rites of the Easter Vigil:

> 1.[7] Already the fragrance of blessedness has come upon you who are being enlightened; already you are gathering "spiritual flowers" for weaving heavenly crowns. Already the Holy Spirit has breathed his secret breath upon you. Already you linger about the forecourt of the royal palace; may you be led in by the king!

In Lecture 16, Cyril properly associates the Holy Spirit with the water of baptism, to show that all the gifts with which Christians are endowed come from the Holy Spirit.

> 16.12[8] Why then did he call water a spiritual grace? Because all things exist from water. It is water which gives life to the green sprouts. Thunder storms send water down from heaven. Water is everywhere the same, but is efficacious in many different ways... So the Holy Spirit, one, the same and undivided, dispenses his grace to each as he wishes. Just as the dry tree, when it receives water begins to bud, so the sinful soul deemed worthy of the Holy Spirit through repentance brings forth clusters of righteousness. At the will of God and in the name of Christ, he dispenses many gifts without losing his simple unity. He employs the tongue of one for wisdom, he

[7]Text: PG 33.332.
[8]Text: PG 33.932.

illuminates the soul of another with prophecy, to another he grants the power to cast out devils, to yet another the interpretation of the Holy Scriptures. One he strengthens in self-control, to one he teaches the deeds of mercy, to another fasting and abstinence, to another contempt of bodily comforts, yet another he prepares for martyrdom. He works in many different ways, yet he is always the same.

But the special gift of the Holy Spirit is enlightenment. Distinguishing the Holy Spirit from evil spirits, Cyril says:

> 16.16[9] Such is not the Holy Spirit. God forbid! On the contrary, the good and the saving are his work. First, his coming is gentle, our perception of him sweet, his burden most light. The rays of his light and knowledge flash forth before his coming. He comes with the concern of a true guardian, for he comes to save and heal, to teach and counsel, to strengthen and encourage, to enlighten the mind, first, of the one who receives him, then through the one, the mind of others. Just as anyone who was once in darkness, then suddenly looks upon the sun, has his bodily eyes lightened and sees clearly what he formerly could not see, so whoever has been thought worthy of the Holy Spirit has his soul enlightened and sees beyond human capability what he did not know. The body is on the earth, yet the soul mirrors the heavens. It sees, with Isaiah, "the Lord sitting upon a throne high and lofty"[Is 6:1], with Ezekiel, "the one who is above the cherubim" [Ez 10.1], and with Daniel "Thousands upon thousands and ten thousands" [Dan 7:10]. The person of no importance sees the beginning of the world and the end of the world, and he knows the intervals of time and the succession of kingdoms—things he never learned in school, for it is the true bearer of the light who is present.

Very shrewdly Cyril weaves into the discourse the behavior expected of one enlightened by the Holy Spirit.

[9]Text: PG 33.940.

16.19[10] If on some occasion when you are sitting in church a conviction comes to you about purity or virginity, this is the teaching of the Holy Spirit. Has it not often happened that a young woman has denied marriage on the very day of her wedding, when the Holy Spirit instructed her about virginity? Is it not true that men who have achieved distinction in the imperial service have rejected wealth and honor at the prompting of the Holy Spirit? Have not young men often seen a beautiful figure, then closed their eyes, refused to look, and so avoided impurity? How can this be, you ask? The Holy Spirit has trained the young man's soul! There is an enormous lust for wealth in the world; why then do Christians live in poverty? Because of the teaching of the Holy Spirit. Truly of great value is the Holy Spirit; quite rightly we are baptized into the name of the Father and of the Son and of the Holy Spirit.

Riding on the crest of enthusiasm, Cyril rises to an eloquent climax:

16.22[11] The Holy Spirit is great and wonderful and all powerful in his gifts. Think how many of you there are who sit here now, how many are gathered together. He directs each appropriately. Being in our midst, he sees the behavior, the thinking and the conscience of each; he knows what we say and think...Think with me of the bishops of each territory, the presbyters, deacons, monks, virgins, and the rest of the laity. Then think of our great patron, the dispenser of gifts. For he is everywhere, and gives to one purity, to another perpetual virginity, to others deeds of mercy, or poverty, or the casting out of evil spirits. And as the one sun lightens all things with its rays, so the Holy Spirit illuminates those who have eyes. If anyone through lack of sight is not thought worthy of his gift, he should not blame the Spirit, but his own unbelief.

[10]Text: PG 33.944.
[11]Text: PG 33.948.

You see the power he exercises throughout the world. Remain no longer then upon the earth but rise to the world above. Ascend, I say, by the power of your mind even to the first heaven and look upon the unnumbered hosts of angels there. Ascend yet further in your thoughts, if you can. Look with me upon the archangels and spirits. See the principalities and powers, authorities, thrones, and dominions. He is before God the master of all these, the teacher, the intercessor who renders them holy.

Tertullian, On the Shows

Cyril was by no means the first to have stressed the importance of the Holy Spirit at baptism, his regenerative power, and his demand for virtuous behavior. It is likely that these were traditional aspects of the message presented to learners and we must pause to observe the theme in the writing of two other Christians. A century and a half before Cyril, Tertullian has written his treatise *On the Shows* to candidates for baptism, in which he claimed that the Holy Spirit was the distinctive possession of the baptized, informing them almost physically, recreating them in mind, and requiring a reformation of behavior appropriate to the image of God in man. He saw the spectacles (in the circus, amphitheatre, theatre and stadium) essentially as the rituals of demons, just as baptism was the ritual of the Holy Spirit. The Holy Spirit required in baptism is a Spirit of gentleness and reason, and quite alien to the madness of the circus. Having shown that the shows are idolatrous, he goes on to say:

> XV[12]... Let us now consider the remaining characteristics of the shows. In every way you will find them contrary to God. God commands us to keep the Holy Spirit within us free from turmoil since it is delicate and

[12]Text: CCL 1.240.

gentle. It is for its good therefore that we keep it calm and undisturbed, quiet and peaceful, and do not molest it with rage, anger, wrath or grief. Will it accommodate itself to the shows? Every show does violence to the spirit. Where there is pleasure, there you will find striving, which gives pleasure direction; where there is striving, there you will find rivalry, which gives point to striving. And where there is rivalry, there you have rage, anger, wrath, grief and the other passions which have no place in the Christian life.

John Chrysostom, Catechetical Instructions

Somewhat later than Cyril, Chrysostom, too, in his catechetical instruction preaches the Holy Spirit as central in the work of regeneration. The textual tradition for Chrysostom's catechetical homilies is highly complex (see bibliographical note), and what follows is selected from the Montfaucon text printed in Migne's *Patrologia.*

> 1.3[13] Take a golden statue which has become marred through the ravages of time and sullied by smoke and ashes and rust, cast it anew and render it pure and shining. In the same way God takes our nature corroded with the rust of sin, darkened by the stains of our transgressions, all its original beauty lost, and casts it anew in his heavenly foundry. He directs a jet of water at the forge; instead of fire he brings the grace of the Holy Spirit; then he takes us out new-fashioned and freshly made to face the bright rays of the sun and so to shine with its brightness. He destroys the old man to make a new man much brighter than the one before.

Like Cyril, Chrysostom teaches that we experience the Spirit above all as the Enlightener:

[13]Text: PG 49.227.

11.1[14]... For this reason, too, you will be called the "newly-enlightened" because, if you wish, the light can always be new for you, and will never be extinguished. Night brings to an end the daily light of our world, whether we wish it or not, but darkness has no knowledge of that heavenly light. "The Light shines in darkness, and the darkness does not repress it" [Jn 1:5]. The earth is bright just so long as the rays of the sun endure. Not so with the soul. It is illuminated and becomes brighter when it receives the gift of the Holy Spirit.

Consider now the comparison more carefully. When night comes and all is dark, one often sees a rope, but thinks it a snake; one flees an approaching friend thinking he is an enemy; one is greatly frightened at any noise. None of this happens during the day, but everything is just as it appears. So it is with our soul. When divine grace comes, it drives away our darkness, and we recognize things for what they are, contemptuous of our former fears. We no longer fear death, for we have learned in these holy rites of initiation that death is not death, but a sleep and a temporary rest. We do not fear poverty, or sickness, or any such thing because we know we are on our way to a better life, pure and incorruptible, and free from all such contingencies.

Did Chrysostom also associate the doctrine of the Holy Spirit with the reform of behavior? Certainly, Chrysostom's message to the learners conveyed a strong imperative for Christian behavior. He reiterates the warning common to catechetical instruction against the spectacles. He forbids oaths, personal adornment, "observance of days, omens and spells"—he calls in fact for an entirely new style of life. And he enjoins the learners already to "practice" the new life style to prepare for the coming of the Spirit. He illustrates with an image from art:

11.3.[15]... Let it be with you as it is with painters. When they have set up their boards, they first trace lightly an

[14]Text: PG 49.233.
[15]Text: PG 49.235.

outline in white of the imperial images to guide them before applying the colors. At this point they have complete freedom to remove and to add: they can erase their mistakes and change what they do not like. But once color is applied, they are no longer able to erase or change, and if they mar the beauty of the picture, the finished work will point its accusing finger at them.

So should it be with you. Think of your soul as the picture. Before you receive in baptism the dye of the Holy Spirit, remove those bad habits deeply ingrained in you—whether your habit of swearing, or lying, or casting insults, or foul talk, or playing the buffoon or anything else equally unacceptable. Obliterate these habits now so that you will not return to them after baptism.

It should be said, however, that in these *Catechetical Instructions* Chrysostom's moral injunctions generally find their rationale less explicitly in the gift of the Holy Spirit at baptism than in the implications of the rituals of baptism and the Eucharist. In baptism Satan is renounced. Hence his pomp—"theatres and the circus, and all sin, and observance of days, and omens and spells" (11.5) — is also renounced. In the Second Instruction, he alludes to various parts of the Eucharist to show their implications for Christian behavior:

> 2.2[16]... Knowing these things, beloved, repay your Benefactor with the practice of a good life. Reflect on the greatness of His sacrifice and so adorn the members of your body. Consider what it is you receive in your hand and do not dare to strike anyone, lest, with a sinful blow, you disgrace the hand honored by such a gift. Consider what you receive and keep your hand clean from greed and plunder. Remember that you not only receive the gift in your hand, but put it to your mouth. Keep your tongue therefore, free from insolent and abusive language, from blasphemy, perjury, and the like. For it is calamitous to

[16]Text: PG 49.233.

3

apply the tongue which has tasted such aweful mysteries, has been reddened by such blood, and become a golden sword, to abuse, and insolence, and ribaldry. Reverence the honor with which God has dignified it, and do not reduce it to the vile conditions of sin. Keep in mind that after hand and tongue, the heart, too, receives that awesome mystery. Do not then ever devise any harm against your neighbor, but keep your mind free from all evil doing. So you shall also be able to guard eyes and ears. How inappropriate, after these mystic words from heaven—I mean the thrice-holy of the cherubim—to defile your ears with lewd songs and suggestive tunes! How truly worthy of that final punishment to use your eyes to look upon harlots when you use them to look upon the aweful and ineffable mysteries, and to commit adultery in your heart.

Cyril of Jerusalem, Catechetical Lectures

We must return now to Cyril of Jerusalem and the lectures given at the very final stage of instruction, during Easter week, after the baptism, the chrism, and the first Eucharist. Cyril (or possibly, John, [cf. above page 221]) refused to expound the meaning of the mysteries to the learners until they had experienced them. With the experience fresh in their minds, he traces the steps in the rituals one by one and explains the significance of each. One point especially commands our attention: the strongly ontological sense in which he views the new life of Christians. During this instruction, Cyril presents a message not merely of a moral transformation, but of an ontological rebirth which takes place in the sacred mysteries. In baptism, one is identified with Christ, in the chrism one is made partaker of the divine nature; so also in the Eucharist, the Body and Blood are so distributed through our physical bodies that we become partakers of the divine nature.

21.2[17] And just as Christ was truly crucified, and buried, and truly rose again, so in baptism you are thought worthy to be crucified with him, to be buried with him, to rise again with him. So also in relation to the chrism. Christ was anointed with the spiritual oil of gladness, that is with the Holy Spirit who is called "the oil of gladness" [Ps 45:7] because spiritual joy comes from him. You too have been anointed with oil, and have become partners of, and participators in, the Anointed One.

Be careful not to suppose that this is mere oil. The bread of the Eucharist after the invocation of the Holy Spirit is no longer mere bread but the Body of Christ. So, this holy oil is no longer merely oil, nor should one call it natural oil after the invocation, but it is the gracious gift of Christ and the Holy Spirit made efficacious through the presence of his divinity. You are anointed sacramentally with oil on your forehead and on other parts of your body, and while the body is being anointed with what appears to be oil, the soul is rendered holy by the holy and life-giving Spirit.

22.3.[18] With full assurance, we participate in the Body and Blood of Christ: in the form of bread, the body is given to you; in the form of wine, the blood is given to you. Thus participating in the Body and Blood of Christ, you may become one body and one blood with Him. So we become "Christ-bearers," for his Body and his Blood have been distributed through the members of our body. As the blessed Peter said, we become partakers of the divine nature [2 Pet 1:4].

The message to learners seems thus to have been carefully adjusted to the stages of instruction. Beginning with the outline of the great events in Saving History, it was at the more advanced stages directed increasingly to the life of the individual, proclaiming a new mode of existence, realized only within the context of the church and through the

[17]Text: SC 126.124.
[18]Text: SC 126.136.

possession of the Holy Spirit understood in quasi-physical terms, and characterized consequently by a radical re-formation of mind and morals.

Suggestions for Further Reading

Easton, Burton S., *The Apostolic Tradition of Hippolytus*, New York 1934, Rp. 1962.

A good introduction, with useful explanatory notes on the catechumenate in the early church.

Harkins, Paul W., *St. John Chrysostom. Baptismal Instructions*, New York 1963.

Recent discoveries (1909 and 1955) of two new series of catechetical instructions have greatly enriched our understanding of Chrysostom's message to learners as represented by the two Instructions from which our selections have been taken. Harkins makes all three series available in translation, and defines the complicated relations among them.

Jungmann, J.A., "Catechumenate" *New Catholic Encyclopedia*, Vol. 3, New York 1967, 238-40.

An excellent brief description of the various stages of instruction given those seeking baptism.

Riley, H.M., *Christian Initiation. A Comparative Study of the Interpretation of the Baptismal Liturgy in the Mystagogical Writings of Cyril of Jerusalem, John Chrysostom, Theodore of Mopsuestia, and Ambrose of Milan*, Washington, 1974.

Riley describes the rites of Christian initiation and explains the meaning they had for four Fathers.

Chapter Seven

THE MESSAGE TO
THE FAITHFUL

The message presented to non-Christians and to learners was by no means irrelevant to Christians, and those who addressed the Christian laity regularly repeated its themes. Indeed, as we have seen, apologetic literature addressed to pagans often assumed that a Christian audience would also be served. In some cases, the defense of Christianity was directed primarily to Christians, to strengthen their faith. It was so with Origen's *Against Celsus* and with the great works of Eusebius of Caesarea, *The Preparation for the Gospel* and *The Defense of the Gospel*. Yet the proclamation of the message to the faithful had to go beyond the themes appropriate to non-Christians, to reveal a fuller range of meaning the Gospel might convey to men and women in the world undertaking to live the life in Christ. A vast store of literature reflects the nature of this message and often gives a delightful view of the manner of its presentation.

The message was presented to the faithful in a myriad of forms. Undoubtedly the most important of these was the homily, delivered by the bishop or a priest on Sundays and festival days. We also have record of a ministry strongly prophetic, sometimes apparently assumed by the laity, in which the message was presented as an oracular word or in visions. At the other end of the spectrum of ecclesiastical order, the message presented to the faithful grew out of the burdens and responsibilities of the episcopal office. The bishop served not only as chief pastor; he could also serve as a judge of disputes (with State authority after Constantine), as an agent of welfare, helping the poor, redeeming captives, while as chief pastor he was responsible for the order and discipline of the churches. Each of his roles provided opportunities to present the message, and we have considerable literature showing how the bishops addressed the faithful. Perhaps none of this literature is more interesting than the Episcopal letters. Finally, whether clerical or lay, the church attracted and produced those who recognized their calling as teachers or writers and approximate our modern scholars and journalists. They, too, were eager to present the message to the faithful, often adapting classical forms to the new themes: philosophical essays, Biblical commentaries, rhetorically shaped treatises, and occasional pamphlets were all used as ways of presenting the message to the faithful. In this chapter we can sample only aspects of three ways in which the message came to the faithful — the Prophetic Vision, the Episcopal letter, and the Scholarly Treatise. I shall not touch on the homily, since an entire volume in this series is devoted to the subject of early Christian preaching.

The Prophetic Vision

"Prophets" appear to have been a familiar part of the New Testament church. Paul speaks in I Corinthians of both the office of prophet and the gift of prophecy:

> *And God has appointed in the church first apostles, second prophets, third teachers, then workers of miracles, then healers, helpers, administrators, speakers in various kinds of tongues. I Cor 12:28*

> *And if I have prophetic powers, and understand all mysteries and all knowledge, and if I have all faith, so as*

> *to remove mountains, but have not love, I am nothing. I Cor 13:2*
>
> *Make love your aim, and earnestly desire the spiritual gifts, especially that you may prophesy. For one who speaks in a tongue speaks not to men but to God; for no one understands him, but he utters mysteries in the Spirit. On the other hand, he who prophesies speaks to men for their upbuilding and encouragement and consolation. I Cor 14:1-3*
>
> *But if all prophesy, and an unbeliever or outsider enters, he is convicted by all, he is called to account by all, the secrets of his heart are disclosed; and so, falling on his face, he will worship God and declare that God is really among you. I Cor 14: 24-25*

In these passages, prophecy has repentance and edification as its main goals. Indeed, Paul contrasts prophecy with tongues, precisely in that its message comes without ambiguity. At the same time there is a suggestion that the prophet was a revealer of mysteries and secrets and the contrast with "tongues" is effective simply because it shares with "tongues," each in its own way, the power of special insight.

It is probable that in the earliest days of the church, the prophetic message was pervasively eschatological: the mysteries revealed were the future events associated with the end of the world. In the event recorded in Acts 11:27, Agabus might originally have been predicting the dire events of the Great Tribulation. Nor did the passing of time entirely destroy the prophetic vision of the end times. The Apocalypse of John, explicitly called a prophecy (Rev 1:3), embodies this message in a powerful moral vision of the world. It seems clear, however, that from a relatively early point, Christians were prepared to give the prophets a wide latitude for their message. The record of Agabus' prophecy is instructive: writing some years after the event, the author has removed every trace of eschatology and moral edification it might once have had, and has made it simply predictive:

> *Now in these days prophets came down from Jerusalem to Antioch. And one of them named Agabus stood up and foretold by the Spirit that there would be a great famine over all the world; and this took place in the days of Claudius. Acts 11:27*

When we meet Agabus a few chapters later, his prophetic stature is enhanced as he undertakes, like the Old Testament prophets, a compelling imitative action, but again the author presents the message as primarily predictive:

> *While we were staying for some days, a prophet named Agabus came down from Judea. And coming to us he took Paul's girdle and bound his own feet and hands, and said, "Thus says the Holy Spirit, 'So shall the Jews at Jerusalem bind the man who owns this girdle and deliver him into the hands of the Gentiles.'" Acts 21:10-11*

From the very earliest times then, the message of the prophets was a characteristic feature of the church. Yet the evidence is that both the understanding of the prophetic role, and the content and character of the message varied enormously. One feature seems to have been commonly shared: an unusual power of vision.

THE TEACHING OF THE TWELVE APOSTLES

This situation does not greatly change in the succeeding centuries. A short section of the *Didache* (*The Teaching of the Twelve Apostles*)—a second century work—allows us to infer a visionary and oracular aspect in the activities of the prophets described there, and a message which is both moral and doctrinal. Unfortunately, the power of prophetic insight was not without abuse:

> 11.7[1] You shall not test or judge any prophet who speaks in the Spirit, for every sin will be forgiven except this. Not everyone who speaks in the Spirit is a prophet,

[1]Text: SC 248.184.

but only the one who follows the ways of the Lord. It is
from their behavior that you can distinguish the false
from the true prophet. When a prophet orders a table in
the spirit, he does not eat from it. If he does, he is a false
prophet. When a prophet does not himself follow the
truth he teaches, he is a false prophet. Every prophet who
has been tested and found true should not be subject to
your judgment when he himself undertakes symbolic
actions signifing the mystery of the church but does not
demand the same of others. God will judge him. Thus
also did the prophets of old. If anyone says in the spirit,
"Give me money," or something else, do not listen to him,
but if he asks you to give for those in need, no one should
judge him.

TERTULLIAN, *ON THE SOUL*

We catch a fascinating view of the manner in which
prophets might present their message in a passage from
Tertullian's *On the Soul*, written in the first years of the
third century.

> IX.4[2] We have a sister among us today who has
> obtained the gift of revelations. These she experiences in
> the church during the liturgy on Sunday when through
> the Spirit she falls into an ecstasy. She speaks with angels,
> sometimes even with the Lord; she sees and hears sacred
> mysteries; she can discern the secret thoughts of some
> people, and she gets remedies for those who need them. It
> is when the Scriptures are being read, or the psalms sung,
> or the sermon preached, or the intercessions made that
> she receives the material for her visions. I happened to be
> making some point about the soul, when this sister was
> "in the Spirit." After the liturgy was finished and the
> people dismissed, she told us, as she usually does, what
> she saw (we scrutinize and test her stories with the great-
> est care). She said, "Among other things, I was shown a

[2]Text: CCL 2.792.

soul in a bodily form, and I saw a spirit, but it was not insubstantial and vacuous. Rather, it was something which could be held, thin and transparent, the color of air, its shape in every way that of a person. This was my vision."

Tertullian's story raises a question about the message this sister normally delivered. There is at least a strong suggestion that it had, at times, a moral and spiritual dimension. But her visions are varied. Tertullian offers not a hint that her medicinal discoveries grew out of a Biblical consciousness of the moral relation between sin and disease. While he finds support in her vision for his own belief in the corporeal nature of the soul, we still cannot avoid the impression that a vision of the color of the soul is both bizarre and theologically insignificant! Like the *Didache*, Tertullian's anecdote reveals an active prophetic ministry in the early church, but one whose message was difficult to control, and often highly idiosyncratic. In this respect, we should not forget that if Paul endeavored to encourage the prophetic ministry to speak a message of moral and spiritual import, the Book of Acts reveals that this message of Christian prophets even in New Testament times could have a very practical and utilitarian focus with no immediate and obvious moral or theological significance. Finally, we should not fail to mark the striking details informing us of the precise way in which the Carthaginian sister received and presented her prophetic message.

HERMAS, *THE SHEPHERD*

The message conveyed by the prophetic vision recorded in *The Shepherd* of Hermas has a stronger moral eschatological intent. *The Shepherd* is possibly a composite work originating about 95 AD when Clement was bishop of Rome, and edited a half-century later. By Tertullian's day (200 A.D.) it had already achieved great honor in the church, for some people regarded practices described by

Hermas as authoritative (Tertullian, *On the Prayer*, 16). Hermas, once a slave, belonged to the Roman church and received visions whose images were of a strongly apocalyptic kind. His chief message is intensely moral but also predictive—a message of repentance in the face of a coming persecution. His message also is rooted in a vivid perception of the power of God both in creating the world and guiding history to its conclusion in the glorification of the church. In the first vision an old woman conveys the message to him:

> 1.3.3[3] Then I listened carefully and heard with amazement what I was not afterwards to recall. For I shuddered at all her words which were such as a man could not bear. But I did remember her final words since they were both expedient and kind: "Behold the God of the powers [the Lord of Hosts] who in his invisible power and might and great wisdom has created the world. With a glorious design, he has conferred beauty upon his creation, by a mighty word he has fixed in place the heavens and established the land above the waters, in his wisdom and foreknowledge he has created his holy church which he has blessed. Behold, he moves the heavens, the mountains, the hills and the seas, and makes all things smooth for his elect, to give them what he promised with great glory and grace. Only they must keep the commandments of God which they received in much faith."

A year later, the same woman appears to him again:

> 11.1.[4] I was on my way to Cumae about the same time as the previous year. As I walked, I recalled the vision of the year before and the spirit caught me up again and took me to the same place. When I arrived there, I fell on my knees and began to pray to the Lord because he had deemed me worthy to make known to me my former sins. After I arose from prayer, I saw before me the old woman whom I had seen a year ago, strolling while she read from a small volume. She said to me, "Are you able to report

[3]Text: SC 532, 84.
[4]Text: SC 532, 88.

these things to God's elect?" I replied, "My lady, I cannot remember so much. Give me the book so I can transcribe it." And she said, "Take it and return it to me." I took it, withdrew further into the field, and transcribed everything letter by letter, for I could not discern the syllables [he was unable to read the book]. When I had completed the work, suddenly someone whom I did not see snatched the book from my hand.

Then I fasted for fifteen days, praying much to the Lord to give me an understanding of the writing. This was what was written: Your children, Hermas, have rejected God and blasphemed the Lord and most wickedly betrayed their parents. They heard themselves called "betrayers of parents" and still they betrayed them though they derived no profit from it. To these sins they added even further—licentiousness and wickedness of all sorts, totally abandoned in their unrestrained lawlessness. Now tell these words to all your children, and to your wife with whom you will henceforth live as a sister. For she, too, sins in that she will not restrain her tongue. Yet when she has heard these words, she will begin to control herself and will find mercy.

After you have told them these words which the Lord has commanded me to reveal to you, all their sins will be forgiven, and indeed the sins all the saints have committed right up to the present day will be forgiven if they repent with their whole heart and remove from their hearts all double-mindedness. For the Lord has sworn by his glory concerning his elect: if they sin after this appointed day, they cannot be saved—there is a limit to repentance for the just. The days of repentance for all the saints have been fulfilled, though there is repentance for pagans until the last day.

Bid also the leaders of the church to make straight their paths in righteousness if they wish to receive fully the promises with great glory. And all you who do righteousness remain steadfast and do not waver and you will have your entrance with the holy angels. Blessed are you who endure the coming great tribulation and do not deny your

> life. The Lord has sworn by his Son that those who deny
> their Lord abandon their lives, that is, those about to
> deny now in the coming days. Those who formerly denied
> have received mercy because of his compassion.

Three points may be briefly noted. First, for all its naiveté,
this vision reflects a much more deeply rooted Biblical
consciousness than we could detect in the vision of the
Carthaginian. Second, the passage suggests a certain tension between the laity and the clergy at Rome. Through the
visionary messenger, Hermas acquires the authority to
declare a general forgiveness of sins to those who repent. An
earnestly moral message from the lips of these prophets
could constitute as serious a danger to ecclesiastical structures as a theologically irrelevant vision. Third, Hermas'
simple prose discloses a touching personal element in the
generation of the vision. He is obviously a man with a
turbulent family life, and his own unhappy domestic situation seems to have provided the cue for a vision of sin and
repentance which he regards as broadly applicable to the
entire church. The prophetic message had its matrix in the
disappointments of his own life.

The Episcopal Letter

The episcopal office placed upon the bishop the responsibility for the welfare of his people, in all the forms such
welfare might assume: physical, moral and spiritual. The
homilies of bishops reveal the concern with which they
addressed the message to every aspect of the life of the laity.
But the bishops of the early church, and especially those of
intellectual stature or political power, found themselves in a
position to catch a synoptic view of the life of the entire
church, and to see the responsibility of their office for the
Catholicity of the church. They had, therefore, not only to
deliver the message within the intimacy of the congregation;
their moral authority might well extend beyond the borders
of their own diocese, and in any case, beyond the reach of

the spoken word. One of the avenues open to them to present the message in these circumstances was the formal letter, written often to a congregation. For this, the New Testament letters of the Apostles provided something of a precedent, though the episcopal letter soon broke away from the form and style of the New Testament epistles. While the subjects of these letters are as manifold as the problems that arose, one theme which persistently appears through the early centuries is that of unity. Conscious of himself on the one hand as the representative of Christ, and on the other as the embodiment of the people of God, a bishop would naturally see the unity of the church as central to its message. A variety of circumstances might evoke an episcopal appeal to this aspect of the message: internecine strife within a neighboring district or diocese, threat of heresy and the persistence of schism, or simply the difficulties caused by party strife in the election of a new bishop. The circumstances eliciting the letters which follow are representative.

CLEMENT OF ROME, *TO THE CORINTHIANS*

Clement, third bishop of Rome in succession to Peter, addressed a letter in the name of the Roman church to the church at Corinth torn by factionalism. The quarrel had grown to a point where a party had undertaken to dismiss some of the clergy. The letter opens with phrases familiar from the Apostolic Epistles, then proceeds at once to address the problem of disunity.

> 1.[5] The church of God which dwells as a stranger in Rome to the church of God which likewise dwells as a stranger in Corinth, to those who have been called and made holy by the will of God through our Lord Jesus Christ. May grace and peace from God who rules over all through Jesus Christ abound toward you.

[5]Text: SC 167.98.

> Because of the misfortunes and calamities which have
> come upon us in sudden succession, brothers, we
> acknowledge that we are somewhat late in turning to the
> matters about which you sought our advice; above all,
> beloved, about the division—strange and foreign to the
> church of God, unholy and defiling—which a few rash
> and presumptuous persons have begun and fanned the
> flames with such utter madness that your name, famous,
> revered and held in high esteem by all, has become the
> subject of great reproach.

In presenting his message, Clement relies heavily on the
highly rhetorical use, well developed by classical authors, of
exempla—examples, or models. In classical theory, *exempla* were widely accepted as an excellent means of persuasion in deliberation about matters of public concern. They
were not regarded in every case as a mere illustration of a
point, but it was understood that the examples at least of
men and women, if portrayed with sufficient power, could
become models which might enter into the hearts and minds
of the listeners to shape their attitudes as in an encounter
with living persons.

Many of Clement's examples are cited to encourage the
virtues of obedience and humility, virtues needed by the
congregation if it were to remain united under the control of
a bishop. He seems to recognize that the imitation of his
models depends upon the reader's keen perception of them:

> 9.2[6] Let us look earnestly upon those who served perfectly his great and shining glory. Let us take Enoch who
> was "translated" because he was found righteous through
> obedience, and was therefore not found by death. Noah
> was found faithful in his service when he proclaimed a
> renewal for the world, and because of him the Lord saved
> the lives of those who went into the ark in unity of heart.
> Abraham, addressed as "friend," was found faithful
> through his obedience to the word of God.[10.] Through
> obedience he left his native land and kinsfolk and father's

[6]Text: SC 167.114, 128.

house, but he left an unimportant country, powerless relatives, and an insignificant house to become heir to the promises of God...

[17.] Let us imitate those who wandered in sheepskins and goatskins preaching the advent of Christ. I mean the prophets Elijah and Elisha, and Ezekiel too, and in addition to them those whose merits God has attested. Abraham received a good report and was called the friend of God. Keeping his eye fixed upon the glory of God, he spoke in humility "I am earth and ashes" [Gen 18:29].

But the great *exemplum* is Christ:

16.[7] He is the Christ of those who have humility, not of those who lift themselves up against his shepherd [the bishop]. For the "Sceptre" of God, our Lord Jesus Christ, did not come with vaunting arrogance and braggadocio, but with humility, as the Holy Spirit had said of him [Clement quotes here Is 53:1-12 and Ps 22:7-9].

You see, beloved, the model given to us. If our Lord thus practiced humility what ought we to do who have through him come under the yoke of his grace?

In Clement's message, the correlatives of obedience and humility are love and forgiveness:

50.[8] You see, beloved, how great and wonderful is love! There is no telling of its perfection. Who is worthy to be found in it except those whom God makes worthy? Let us pray and seek his mercy that we should be found in love, blameless and without human partiality. All the generations from Adam to the present have passed away, but those who have been made perfect in love through the grace of God have their dwelling among the godly. These shall be revealed in the manifestation of the Kingdom of God... For our transgressions, then, and for what we have done at the instigation of our adversary, let us ask to be forgiven.

[7]Text: SC 167.124.
[8]Text: SC 167.180.

The themes of love and humility adumbrated here in a message to the faithful, were to be re-echoed in other contexts as a central aspect of the Christian message. In the message to the pagans Tertullian, as we have seen, was to find in the theme of Christian love a focus for his climactic portrait of Christian society, while for Augustine, the fundamental contrast between the heavenly and the earthly cities is that of pride and humility.

The Biblical *exempla* in Clement's Letter serve a further function we should not overlook. They provide much of the material for the pattern of Saving History which Clement weaves in a somewhat desultory manner into his work. The patriarchs, the prophets, Christ are examples for our imitation. They also recall God's saving acts in history. Clement completes the pattern by images of the resurrection and Judgment. Clement saw that Christian unity had its theological foundation in Saving History. The point has some importance. The message of love and humility appropriate to this particular situation was not to be divorced therefore from the events of Saving History. We should recall that Saving History was the theme of Peter's first sermons to the Jews in Acts, while Augustine would make it the theme of the instructor's message to the Catechumens. It is to say that "Saving History" remains the message, par excellence, of the Christian.

We must note, finally, that Clement's Letter carries an argument pervasive in early Christian thought, that the bishop stands in a line of succession originating with God's mandate to Christ, Christ's to the Apostles, and the Apostles' to those who succeeded them. Clement presents the case succinctly:

> 42.[9] The Apostles received the Gospel from the Lord Jesus Christ, and Jesus Christ was sent from God. Thus Christ is from God and the apostles from Christ. Both proceeded from the will of God in a proper order. The Apostles received their commission fully assured by the

[9]Text: SC 167.168.

resurrection of our Lord Jesus Christ. Believing the word of God they went forth with the assurance of the Holy Spirit, preaching the coming Kingdom of God. Declaring the message in town and country, they appointed their first converts, once tested, as bishops and deacons of those who would come to believe. This was not new, for long ago it had been written concerning bishops and deacons: "I shall appoint their bishops in righteousness and their deacons in faith" [Is 60:17]. . .

44.[10] The Apostles knew through our Lord Jesus Christ that dissension would arise over the name of bishop. For this reason, when they had received perfect knowledge, they appointed the aforesaid, and afterwards provided that, if they should pass away, others well approved were to assume their office. Those then who were appointed by the apostles, or later by other esteemed men with the approval of the whole church, who have served faithfully the flock of Christ with humility and care, who in the course of time have acquired a good reputation, one cannot justly deprive of their office.

IGNATIUS OF ANTIOCH

It is with Ignatius of Antioch, a contemporary of Clement, that this argument becomes a focal point in the message of Christian unity. Ignatius was bishop of Antioch in Syria, but we come to know him through the letters he wrote to churches in Asia. He had been apprehended in Antioch as a Christian and was traveling under guard through Asia on his way to suffer martyrdom in Rome. Delegations from several churches in Asia, among them those of Ephesus and Tralles, met him and evidently from these he learned that a form of gnosticism was disrupting the unity of the churches. His message to all these churches strikes a common note: the members must remain with the bishop, for where the bishop is, there is the church.

[10]Text: SC 167.172.

To the Ephesians

1.1[11] I have learned of the name much beloved in God which you have acquired through your righteous character through faith and love in Jesus Christ our Savior. As imitators of God, kindled anew through the blood of God, you have performed perfectly a kinsman's deed. For when you heard that I was on my way from Syria bound on behalf of our common name and hope, and that I hoped through your prayers to fight wild beasts in the Roman amphitheatre—for thus I may become a disciple—you hastened to make enquiry. Now in the person of Onesimus your bishop, a man whose love is beyond telling, I have received your whole congregation in the name of God. I pray that you all love your bishop in Jesus Christ, and that you all imitate him. Blessed is He who has granted you to be worthy of such a bishop...

Thus you ought to agree with the mind of your bishop, as indeed you do. For your distinguished presbyters, worthy of God, are in harmony with your bishop, like the strings of a lyre. Therefore in your concord and harmonious love Jesus Christ is sung. You then be the chorus so that you employ a divine scale, and sing to the Father in oneness of mind with the unity of a single voice through Jesus Christ. The Father will hear you and recognize that insofar as you do well, you are the members of his Son. It is good for you to dwell in blameless unity and so always to participate in God.

If I in this short time have enjoyed so much fellowship with your bishop, a fellowship not of a merely human sort, but spiritual, how much more do I count you happy who are so closely united to the bishop, as the church is to Christ, and Christ is to the Father, that all may be harmonious in unity. Make no mistake. If anyone excludes himself from the altar, he is deprived of the bread. If the prayer of one or two has such great strength, how much

[11]Text: SC 10.68.

more the prayer of the bishop and the whole church. Whoever does not come to the common assembly is proud and judges himself, for it is written, "God withstands the proud" [Prov 3:34]. Let us take care then not to withstand the bishop so that we may be subject to God.

To the Trallians

2.[12] For whenever you are subject to the bishop as to Jesus Christ, you appear to me to be living not according to man, but according to Jesus Christ who died for us that you might escape death by believing on his death. As you now do, it is essential that you continue to do nothing apart from the bishop. Be subject also to the presbyters as to the Apostles of Jesus Christ our hope, for if we have lived in him, we shall be found in him. Those who serve the mysteries of Jesus Christ [the deacons] must in every way be pleasing to all. For they are not dispensers of food and drink, but servants of the Church of God. They must therefore guard themselves from blameworthy actions, as they would keep themselves from fire.

Likewise, all must show respect for the deacons as for Jesus Christ, for the bishop is a type of the Father, the presbyters of the council of God and the fellowship of the Apostles. Apart from these, you do not have the church.

CYPRIAN, *LETTERS*

Cyprian of Carthage became bishop only about a year before the Decian persecution broke in 250 A.D. Cyprian himself was forced to flee, and he endeavored to direct his church from his hiding place. But his absence created turmoil in the Carthaginian church. Cyprian refused an easy reconciliation to the lapsed, and a party soon arose in

[12]Text: SC 10.112.

opposition to him, which received the support of some of the martyr-confessors. In a letter to them, Cyprian declares passionately that the evangelical message cannot countenance schism:

> XLVI.[13] From Cyprian to Maximus and Nicostratus and the other confessors: Greetings.
>
> Since you have often had occasion to learn from my letters in what honor I hold your confession and what love I have towards your close-knit fellowship, believe and accept this letter, I beg you, in which I am writing to you plainly about my concern for you as well as for your actions and the praises you have won. For I am grieved and saddened, indeed, seized with almost unbearable anguish of heart, to learn that you have conspired to create another bishop, against ecclesiastical rules, contrary to the law of the Gospel, opposed to the unity of the Catholic church. That is to say, you have done what is neither right nor permitted, for you have set up another church, you have torn apart the body of Christ, you have mangled the soul and body of the Lord's flock with rival loyalties. I ask that in you at least that unlawful division of our brotherhood should not persist, but that you remember your confession and the sacred tradition, and return to the mother you left, who rejoiced so much in the glory of your confession. Do not imagine that you are declaring the gospel of Christ as long as you stand apart from the flock of Christ and from his peace and concord. It is much better for soldiers who have achieved distinction and fame to remain within their own camp, and there to consider and plan for the common undertaking. We must never destroy our unity and concord. And since we ourselves cannot leave the church, walk out of its doors and come to you, we beg and beseech you, with all the persuasion at our command, that you return to our fellowship and to our common mother, the church. Our very best wishes, dear brothers.

[13]Text: CSEL III.2.604.

For Cyprian the Gospel was to be found in the Catholic church, and the unity of the church was thus central to its message. Indeed, Cyprian's best known work, a treatise *On the Unity of the Church*, makes the same claims as the letter above, and elaborates upon the theology so briefly enunciated here.

AUGUSTINE, *LETTERS*

It was little more than half a century after Cyprian that the African church was torn apart by what is perhaps the most famous schism of antiquity, that of the Donatists. The Donatists took their name from Donatus, the first bishop (from 313-355) of importance in the Donatist church. The schism had arisen from the claim of the Donatists that one of the bishops who in 311/312 consecrated Caecilian as bishop of Carthage had surrendered the Scriptures to the authorities in the recent persecution of Diocletian. The Donatists held to the main points of Catholic doctrine, and constituted therefore not a heresy but a schism, a schism motivated by a determination to maintain the purity of the church. The Donatists prospered throughout the 4th century, in spite of imperial opposition. As we have seen, they seem to have been a considerably larger body than the Catholics in Augustine's own Hippo Regius, and they often used violence to menace the Catholics. For more than a decade Augustine struggled against the Donatists, and consequent upon a conference of Catholics and Donatists in Carthage in 411, the imperial arm was raised against them. Throughout these years he reflected much, though in the heat of battle, on the nature of schism and the appropriate response to it. Two letters are indicative of positions he came to reach.

In our first example, we can see Augustine struggling with the problems of coercion. At an early stage in his battle with the Donatists, Augustine thought that persuasion, not force, was the only appropriate means to achieve unity. But as the struggle wore on, Augustine became convinced that the church's appeal to schismatics should be reinforced by pressure from the government: the episcopal message of unity was to be effected by secular power. Augustine is not completely comfortable and in the following letter to the Donatists, intended for general circulation, he charges that they have brought the imperial arm against themselves:

> 105[14] The love of Christ for which we wish to gain all people, as far as we can, does not permit us to be silent. If you hate us because we preach to you a Catholic peace we only serve the Lord who said, "Blessed are the peacemakers for they shall be called the sons of God" (Mt 5:9), while it was written in the Psalms, "I was peaceful towards those who hate peace; when I spoke to them they made war upon me for no reason" (Ps 120:7).
>
> Some of your presbyters have given us orders in words like this: "Leave our people alone if you do not want us to kill you." How much better for us to reply: "Do not you leave our people alone, but rather approach in peace, not indeed our people, but the people of Him to whom we all belong. If you do not wish to do this, but to remain hostile, then leave the people alone for whom Christ shed his blood. You wish to make them yours so that they should not belong to Christ, although you try to get possession of them under his name. If a slave steals sheep from his master's flock, he puts his master's brand on them and their lambs to conceal his theft. So your predecessors did: they separated from the Church of Christ the people who had the baptism of Christ and baptized again with the baptism of Christ both those themselves and their converts. But the Lord punishes thieves who do not amend their ways, and calls back to his flock the wandering sheep, and does not destroy the mark he has branded upon them. . . .
>
> If you dislike us because you are being coerced into our unity by imperial orders, remember that you have

[14]Text: CSEL 34.595.

brought this upon yourselves. For whenever we wished to preach the truth you have never allowed anyone to be free to hear it or make his own choice, because of the violence and terrorism you have stirred up. Stop screaming and calm yourselves. Consider quietly, if you can, what we are saying, and ponder again the deeds of your circumcellions [country brigands] and your clergy who are inevitably their leaders. Then you will see why imperial orders have been issued against you. Your complaint is unfair, because you yourselves have coerced the government to issue these orders."

In our second example, likewise an "open letter" to the Donatists, Augustine considers the problem of schism from a theological point of view.

76.1[15] The Catholic church says to you Donatists: "Children of men, how long will you be slow to perceive? Why do you love falsehood and seek a lie?" (Ps 4:2). Why do you separate yourselves from the unity of the whole world by an abominable and sacrilegious schism? You pay attention to the false things people say to you, whether deliberately or by mistake, about the surrender of the Scriptures, to keep you in heretical separation. You do not pay attention to what the Scriptures themselves say to win you to Catholic peace. Why do you listen to those who say what they could never prove, while you are deaf to the Word of God who says: "You are my Son. Today have I begotten you. Ask me, and I shall give you the peoples for your inheritance, and the ends of the earth as your possession" (Ps 2:7-8)? "The promises were given to Abraham and to his seed. He does not say 'seeds,' as though speaking of many, but of one: 'to your seed,' which is Christ" (Gal 3:16). "In your seed," he says, "all peoples will be blessed" (Gen 22:18). Lift up the eyes of your heart and consider the whole world, how all peoples are blessed in the seed of Abraham. Formerly, one

[15]Text: CSEL 34.324.

believed what was not yet seen; now you see, and still look askance. The passion of the Lord is the price of the whole world; he bought back the world. Yet you are not in concord with the world—to your gain—but rather to your loss stand apart and struggle to destroy the whole. Hear in the Psalm at what cost we have been redeemed: "They pierced my hands and my feet. They counted all my bones. They looked upon me and observed. They divided my clothing among themselves and cast lots for my garments" (Ps 22:18, 19). Why do you wish to divide the garment of the Lord, and do not wish to hold in common with the world that seamless cloak of charity?...

You imagine that you are removing yourselves from the weeds before the harvest of the wheat, but you alone are the weeds. If you were grain you would endure the sprinkling of weeds and not separate yourself from the planting of Christ. Concerning the weeds, it is said, "Unrighteousness will abound and the love of many will grow cold," but of the wheat, "Whoever endures to the end will be saved" (Mt 24:12, 13). Why do you believe that weeds have sprung up and filled the world, while the wheat has disappeared to remain only in Africa? You say you are Christians, you contradict Christ. He himself said, "Leave both to grow until harvest" (Mt 13:30)—he did not say, "Let the weeds increase but the grain decrease." He said, "The field is this world" (Mt 13:38)— he did not say "The field is Africa." He said "The harvest is the end of the world" (Mt 13:39)—he did not say, "The harvest is the time of Donatus."

Augustine concludes his letter by an appeal to the seamy side of Donatist history where the Donatists' deeds convict them of the same charges they make against the Catholics. From a theological point of view, Augustine's message is clear: the Gospel calls for a Catholic church, not a pure church. The test of the true church is Catholicity, not purity, the demand made upon its members' love, not sinlessness.

The Scholarly Treatise

One of the issues which the early church faced, and which indeed is with us today, was: "How far can the message bear exploration? How far can its presentation undergo experimentation to find new forms?" While these are questions germane to every Christian, they often achieve a special poignancy in the reflection of scholars. The modern scholar searches to explore the significance of the message, to find language and forms in which to express its fullness, to present it in its wholeness. A tension often arises between the security of the tradition and the idiosyncracies of the perceptions of individual scholars. It was a tension not unknown to the early church, and it will be appropriate to conclude this study of the Message and Its Presentation, by turning to several writers who addressed the problems arising from the need and desire of the faithful to explore the message. Three of these are men of the late second and early third centuries—Tertullian, Clement of Alexandria, and Origen. Clement and Origen, as we have seen, were both teachers with some equivalence perhaps to college professors today. In some respects, Tertullian was rather more a pamphleteer than a scholar, but he was immensely learned in the literature, philosophy and medicine of his day, and he is still regarded by many critics as the first Latin-speaking theologian of the West. We shall consider treatises in which they themselves intend to share with the faithful their own perceptions of the message, but we shall not attempt to describe the content of their message. We must be satisfied rather to observe them as they consider the question of the nature and limits of its exploration. More than a century later, a fourth figure, Gregory of Nazianzus, faced the problem in a somewhat different context, and some citations from his work will offer points of comparison with the earlier writers.

TERTULLIAN,
On The Prescription Against Heretics

Tertullian's most forceful statement about the duty and the right of the faithful to explore the message appears in the introduction to his treatise *On the Prescription Against Heretics*. Although Tertullian wrote individual treatises to confute individual heresies, he attempted in this work to provide the equipment to withstand all heresies. It is thus an exposition of the nature of heresy in general. Tertullian believes that willful "curiosity" lies at the root of heresy, and in his introduction he bitterly attacks investigation for its own sake, since curiosity is the chief enticement to heresy. Faced with the challenge that the dominical words charge us to seek in order to find, he undertakes to explain the limits of exploration.

> 10.[16] Now the meaning of this statement ["Seek and you shall find" (Mt 7:7)] rests on three points: subject, time, and measure. In relation to subject you consider what is to be sought; in relation to time, when; in relation to measure, to what extent. You are to seek therefore that which Christ established, to seek as long as you have not found, and until you have found. But you found it when you believed, for you would not have believed if you had not found, just as you would not have sought except to find. Thus in seeking to find, and in finding to believe you have, by believing, established the extent of seeking and finding. The very result of seeking has defined the measure for you. He himself established this boundary who does not want you to believe anything else than what he has taught and so not to seek for anything else.

Yet Tertullian agrees that within the limits of what Christ has taught, investigation is appropriate to the Christian, provided he recognizes that it is faith which saves. Tertullian compendiously defined the teachings of Christ by what he

[16]Text: CCL 1.195.

calls "The Rule of Faith," whose content is virtually identical to the Apostles' creed.

> 12.[17] Our exploration must always go just so far. But where should we explore? Among heretics where all is foreign and opposed to the truth we possess, people whom we are forbidden to approach?... Let us search therefore within what is our own, under the guidance of our own, and about what is our own. This we may do on any matter arising for investigation provided the "Rule of Faith" is not threatened... For this "Rule," as I shall show, was established by Christ and raises no questions for us except those which heresies throw up and make heretics. But if the "Rule" remains firm in its proper place you may explore, and investigate, indeed, satisfy your passionate curiosity, all you like. If you think you have discovered an ambiguity somewhere or a dark mystery find some brother [to help you] who is a scholar deeply learned, or someone who has studied and is like yourself curious and yet seeking.

On The Veiling of Virgins

In a slightly later work, under the prophetic and charismatic influence of Montanism, Tertullian affirmed that while the central truth of the Rule of Faith never changes, yet the Spirit reveals to the constantly increasing awareness of the church the significance of the Gospel message.

> 1.3[18] There is indeed only one Rule of Faith; it alone cannot be changed or reformed... Keep this Rule of Faith secure, then other aspects of the discipline and of our behavior admit change and improvement, for the grace of God continues to work and advances right to the end. Is one to imagine that when the Devil is forever working and daily adding to the devices of evil, the work

[17]Text: CCL 1.197.
[18]Text: CCL 2.1209.

---

of God has ceased or failed to make progress? Since, moreover, our human capacity was not able to receive the divine fullness all at once, the Lord sent the Paraclete so that the discipline might gradually be directed, ordered and brought to perfection by the Holy Spirit, that "vicar" of the Lord... What then is the administrative work of the "vicar" Paraclete except this, to direct discipline, reveal the Scriptures, reform the understanding, to lead to better things?

In this passage Tertullian formulates a theological foundation for the development of ecclesiastical tradition. The Christian mind, enlightened by the Spirit, must draw from the message its implications for the expanding life of the church. The message remains constant in its fundamental themes; but it steadily grows in the richness of its significance and in the breadth of its applicability to our lives.

ORIGEN, *ON FIRST PRINCIPLES*

In his work *On First Principles*, it was Origen's intent to systematize the great truths of the Christian message, both by organizing the Christian teaching into a logical structure, and by bringing to the message a systematic demonstration based both on the evidence of logical argument and the appeal to Scripture. His work was, in effect, a scholarly exposition of the message. As a scholar, he recognized that his explorations must begin at, but go well beyond, the universally accepted teachings of the church. In his Preface, he justifies the need for scholarly exploration.

1 Praef.[19] All who believe and are assured that grace and truth have come through Jesus Christ, [Jn. 1.17] and know that Christ is the truth, as he himself said ("I am the truth" [Jn 14:6]), receive the knowledge which calls men to living the good, that is the blessed, life, from no other source than the very words and teaching of Christ...

[19]Text: SC 252.76.

2. Yet many who profess to believe Christ disagree not only on small and insignificant matters, but also on major important isues. They disagree, for example, about God, about the Lord Jesus Christ, about the Holy Spirit; and not only about these but about other beings which have been created, for example the "principalities and powers." It seems necessary, therefore, first to lay down fixed limits and a clear rule about each of these things, and then to investigate other matters. There are many among both Greeks and barbarians who promise truth, but we no longer seek it among those who affirm it falsely once we believe that Christ is the Son of God and know that we must learn the truth from Him. Similarly, since there are many who think they understand the things of Christ, but in some cases differ from their predecessors, we must maintain the teaching of the church duly handed down in succession from the Apostles right to the present day. We must believe only that truth which in no respect disagrees with the ecclesiastical and apostolic tradition.

3. Now what the holy Apostles believed essential, this they handed down with conspicuous clarity even to those who were somewhat slow to investigate theology. The principles underlying their assertions, however, they left for the exploration of those who should merit the distinguished gifts of the Spirit and would receive through the Spirit himself the gifts of speech, wisdom and knowledge. The Apostles spoke about other matters, too, declaring the reality of certain things, but saying nothing about their mode and source. Obviously they intended that future scholars eager for wisdom should have some field of activity in which to display the fruits of their ability. They meant those scholars who would prepare themselves to be worthy and capable of receiving wisdom.

CLEMENT OF ALEXANDRIA, *MISCELLANIES*

Perhaps the most interesting discussion from a scholar's pen on the Message and Its Presentation comes from Clement. We have three major works from Clement, the *Exhortation to the Greeks*, which we considered in chapter 3, the *Instructor*, and the *Miscellanies*. In the *Instructor*, Clement says that the Divine Word first exhorts, then trains, and finally teaches, a sequence which would seem to correspond to the intent of the three major works. It would be wrong to define narrowly the audience for any of these works: Clement clearly envisions pagan readers for his *Miscellanies*; but at the same time, the goal of the *Miscellanies* is to address the Christian gnostic. For Clement, the Christian gnostic is one who has grown in understanding and faith through hard intellectual labor to the point where he can discern the hidden truths of God, where he understands, that is, the message in its fullest significations. He is implicitly contrasted with the heretical gnostics who claimed a knowledge of the divine mysteries by virtue not of investigation but of their nature, which by good fortune contained a spark of divinity allowing them immediate insights into, and participation in, the divine.

Faced with the gnostic challenge that the saving truth came through one's nature as a lucky circumstance of birth, Clement repeatedly insists that on the contrary, the truth of the message can be discovered only by investigation, by hard work. He refuses to recognize a radical discontinuity between the knowledge of philosophy and the knowledge of the hidden truths of Christianity. Consequently Clement insists that both the common sense of philosophy and the enigma of mystical truth must be part of the presentation of the message. Philosophy is the shell which on the one hand protects the interior secrets suitable only for the nourishment of the faithful, and on the other entices the true and Christian gnostic to the delectable meat of revelation.

> 1.1.17[20]. . . . Just as farmers prepare the land by irrigation, so we water the soil with the river of Greek learning so that it might receive the spiritual seed cast upon it and

[20]Text: GCS 15.12 (=SC 30.56).

nourish it well. These *Miscellanies* contain the truth mingled with, or rather, hidden and concealed by, the doctrines of philosophy, as the meat of a nut is concealed by the shell. For I think it appropriate that the kernels of truth should be reserved for the "farmers of faith" alone. I am not unaware of the objections of some ignorant and timid people who say that one should concern himself with the essentials, the things that build up faith, that secular learning is superfluous, wearies us to no purpose, and occupies our time without contributing anything to our goal. They think that philosophy has unfortunately come upon our life as the plague of mankind, devised by some diabolical agent. But throughout all these *Miscellanies* I shall show that what is evil has an evil nature and no farmer would suppose it is something good and shall suggest that philosophy, too, is in some way the work of divine foresight.

1.11.20[21] Philosophy came into existence to give us the fruit of knowledge when we receive a sure grasp of the truth through the scientific demonstration of things assumed. I say nothing of the fact that the *Miscellanies* have been deliberately shaped to reflect a broad acquaintance with scholarship with the intent of skillfully hiding the kernels of knowledge. Like a keen hunter who seeks out, tracks down, explores, chases, then catches his quarry, so the truth seems to be something sought for its sweetness but caught through labor.

VI.1.2.[22] . . . Thus my notes might kindle a fire both in myself and in those who are ready for knowledge, if indeed it finds those who are ready to search with diligent labor for what is fitting and useful. For it is right that those who are being led to the eternal and blessed salvation should undergo a labor not for food but much rather for knowledge, since "the way of the Lord is narrow and confined" (Mt 7:14).

[21] Text: GCS 15.14 (=SC 30.59).
[22] Text: GCS 15.423.

Further, the message must be presented to the faithful in the form of "scientific demonstration," based on faith:

> II.XI.48[23] Faith is knowledge defined as the scientific demonstration of doctrines handed down in accordance with the true philosophy. We might say that knowledge is a process of reasoning from what is acknowledged to what is in dispute and which results in faith.
>
> ...For the highest demonstration which we have referred to as "scientific" produces, through the study and disclosure of the Scriptures, faith in those who are eager to learn, and this is knowledge.

We must note finally that for Clement the responsibility of the "true gnostic" is not merely to present the message as a mode of intellectual exploration. The growth into perfect wisdom comes through an exemplary coordination of deeds with words: one mediates the truth he lives. Hence, the message must be presented in such a way as to enable the hearers to grow into the very likeness of God:

> VI.XV.115[24] The gnostic, then, receives an exact impress, the very mind of the Teacher, the thoughts He had when He gave commandments and counsel to the wise and prudent. The gnostic understands this mind as the Teacher wished, for he has grown into it through a fitting process of thought. On the one hand, he has taught with distinction upon the house-tops those who are able to build their houses aloft [he has taught deep truths to those able to receive them]; on the other, he has been the first to put into practice what he has taught as an example in daily life, for he has taught what can be done. He understands that he who is a Christian and thus bears the name of king possesses power and has control. For we have not been ordered to be lords merely over the beasts of the fields, but over our own wild passions also...
>
> Thus the gnostic knows how to present the message— when, in what way, and to whom.

---

[23]Text: GCS 15.138.
[24]Text: GCS 15.489.

VII.IX.52[25] Whoever assumes the responsibility for the instruction of others extends yet further the honor of the gnostic, for he has received the stewardship both in word and deed of the greatest good on earth—a stewardship by which he mediates participation in and union with the divine...For everything he has in his mind he expresses in his speech, addressing those worthy to hear and living life in harmony with his words.

VII.X.57[26]...Faith is, so to speak, a compendious knowledge of the essential matters. Knowledge is a firm and secure demonstration of what has been received through faith. It is built on faith through the teachings of the Lord and leads to the unchangeable which we grasp with the understanding. It seems to me that the first step in salvation is the conversion from paganism to faith, but the second step is the change from faith to knowledge. This, carried forward into love, here in this world makes the one who knows beloved by the one who is known and loved. Soon such a person already in anticipation is able in this world to be like the angels. And after he has drawn his last breath, then changing for the better he shall hasten through the sacred heavens to his Father's dwelling place to be with his Lord, evermore an abiding light, at last in every way absolutely unchangeable.

We must yet glance at a problem germane to our whole subject of the presentation of the message and which surfaces with some feeling in the *Miscellanies*. Clement knows of those who are strongly critical of any attempt to present the message by the written word. The message should be conveyed only by the voice, and through the presence of the living person. There is a hint, further, that even in Clement's day publication was sought for the glory it bestowed upon the scholar, and the motive was seen as wholly inappropriate for the messenger of the gospel. Clement diplomatically justifies the "book" as a medium for the message while defending both the spoken voice and the written word:

[25]Text: GCS 17.38.
[26]Text: GCS 17.42.

1.1.4[27] If two preach the word, one through writing and one through speech, are not both to be accepted, since they both make faith active through love?... Both the herald and the messenger bring news. It makes no difference how it comes, whether by hand or mouth, if it brings aid... The one who speaks to those who are present tests and judges them and distinguishes the person able to hear from the others. He pays attention to words, manners, character, life, movements, attitudes, glance and voice. He watches for the crossroads, the stony ground, the open road, the fruitful land, the places overgrown with wood, the fertile and cultivated soil, able to bring forth abundant crops. But the one who speaks through books, prepares himself before God and cries out that he may not write for gain or glory, nor in writing become the dupe of prejudice, the slave of fear, or the victim of pleasure, but may gain only the salvation of those who read. He receives no reward in the present but in hope awaits payment from him who has promised to give to his workers the wages they deserve.

GREGORY OF NAZIANZUS, *THEOLOGICAL ORATIONS*

The prerogatives of the faithful receive a further discussion in Gregory (ca. 330-390) who spent much of his life at Nazianzus in Cappadocia where for a brief period he succeeded his father as bishop. But he was invited by the orthodox minority in Constantinople to help reorganize their church, and soon became a very popular preacher in the capital. Because the city was largely Arian, he undertook to explain and defend Nicene orthodoxy. In 380 he preached the famous "Five Theological Orations," in which he set out the Christian understanding of God and the Holy Trinity in accordance with the Nicene definition, and

[27]Text: GCS 15.4 (=SC 30.46).

against the Arians. He devotes his first Oration to our
present question: under what circumstances may a theologian discuss the question of God? The question gained a
special force from the circumstances in which Gregory
spoke. Under Valens, Emperor in the East from 364 to 378,
Arianism had had imperial approval in Constantinople and
was thus in a position of great strength. Moreover, after half
a century of heated, sometimes violent, debate the discussion of God had become, according to Gregory, a pastime
even for the masses. Yet Gregory's answer to the question
stands within the tradition established by Tertullian, Clement and Origen: exploration of the message is the Christian's obligation, but limits must be observed. Above all, the
heart and mind of those who discuss must be prepared and
thus become worthy to consider the sacred truths of Christian faith. At this point, Gregory is clear and forceful and
needs little interpretation. We may therefore conclude this
chapter with his own words:

> 27.3[28] It does not belong to everyone with all due
> respect, to philosophize about God. This is no small
> matter, and it belongs to those who approach in humility.
> It is not appropriate to discuss God at all times, nor with
> all people, nor all aspects of the subject, but there is a
> proper time, the right people, and a sufficient extent.
>
> It does not belong to all, just because it belongs to those
> who have been carefully tested and have advanced far in
> speculation; indeed before even this they have cleansed
> themselves in body and soul, or to be more precise, are
> cleansing themselves. We must not attempt to grasp the
> pure with the impure, just as it is not without danger to
> look upon the sun's rays with a diseased eye.
>
> What then is the proper time? When we are free from
> the defilement and confusion of the outside world, and
> our mind is not troubled with false and perverse images,
> as though beautiful calligraphy were to be mixed with
> bad writing, or the fragrance of perfume with the stench

[28]Text: SC 250.76.

of the sewer. To know God, one must have true leisure. We can make judgments about theology when we find the appropriate time.

And who are the right people with whom to discuss? Those surely for whom it is a serious matter, and not just one of many things they like to talk about, chattering pleasant nonsense after the circus, theatre, and concert, after dinner, or indeed after the brothel. Those are not the right people who enjoy polite argument for its own sake.

Finally, about what subjects and to what extent are we to philosophize? We should discuss those things that are within our reach and to the extent that the listener is able and willing to hear, not like women who overwhelm us with an extravagance of words or dainties to the detriment of our ears or our bodies. To take other analogies, the greatest burdens weigh down beyond their strength the beasts that bear them, and the heaviest rains flood the earth. So these too are burdened by the difficulty of the words and lose even their original strength.

I do not mean that we should not in every possible way think about God—for I should not want anyone to dog us on that score. It is more important that we think of God than that we breathe. If I may say so, we ought to do nothing else. I am among those who approve the Word which exhorts us to attend to Him day and night [Ps 1:2], to speak of Him in the evening and in the morning and at noon [Ps 55:16-17], and to bless the Lord at all times [Ps 34:1]—in the words of Moses [Deut 6:7] when one goes to bed, gets up, travels, or does anything at all, he ought to be forming himself by his recollection after the pattern of purity. So I do not forbid constant reflection, but only theologizing. Nor do I prevent theology as though it were an irreverent investigation but only when it is inappropriate. I do not prevent teaching, but only excess. Too many sweets bring nausea, however good the sweets; and there is a time for everything, as Solomon thought, and as I think, too. Beauty is not beauty when the effect is not beautiful—for example a flower is quite out of place in the winter; the adornment of a man is inappropriate on a woman, or of a woman on a man; one does not discuss geometry in the midst of a friend's misfortune; tears have no place at a drinking party. Is it only in the case of theology that we shall disregard propriety, when theology above all requires a sense of what is fitting?

Suggestions for Further Reading

von Campenhausen, H., *Ecclesiastical Authority and Spiritual Power in the Church of the First Three Centuries*. Trans. J.A. Baker, Stanford 1969.

Chapters 7 and 8 reveal how the message came to find its validation in the office of bishop rather than in the visions of the prophets.

Grant, Robert M. (ed), *The Apostolic Fathers. A New Translation and Commentary*, New York 1964—1968.

Six volumes by different authors. Volume 1 (Grant) is a general introduction. Writings mentioned in this chapter: *1 Clement*, Vol. 2 (Grant); *Didache*, vol. 3 (Kraft); *Ignatius*, vol. 4 (Grant); *Hermas*, vol. 6 (Snyder).

Hinchliff, P., *Cyprian of Carthage and the Unity of the Catholic Church*, London 1974.

Shows how Cyprian's theology gradually changed in response to the needs of unity within the church.

Richardson, C.C., *The Christianity of Ignatius of Antioch*, New York 1935.

A useful chapter (pages 33-40) expounds Ignatius' conception of unity.

Reiling, J., *Hermas and Christian Prophecy. A Study of the Eleventh Mandate*, Leiden 1973.

A thorough study of the phenomenon of prophecy in the church of the second century.

CONCLUSION

In the preceding chapters, I have tried to offer a description rather than an argument. It has not been my intent to illustrate a theory, or theories, about the nature and content of the message, or about its presentation. If the early Christians were to speak for themselves, my task was rather to gather up and organize the evidence, with sufficient commentary to enable the reader to acquire the context necessary to hear and understand their words. I have included passages because they were relevant to our subject (and interesting), not because they added weight to a thesis. There can be no question, at this point, therefore, of an inclusive summary of "results." It is the words of the Fathers—whatever they may say—which are important, and to these the reader must return. At the same time, a few concluding observations will not be amiss.

In the first place, one can only be deeply impressed by the profound reflection and vigorous discussion of the early Christians on the problem of method—how to present the message. On the one hand, we can discern this reflection in the deliberate choice of the structure and form of literary works. For presenting the message to the Jews, Justin Martyr validates the dialogue, understood as "opening the Scriptures," by introducing a contrasting dialogue in the Platonic manner, and by subtle hints recalling the model of our Lord's post-resurrection dialogue with two Jews on the road to Emmaus. Minucius Felix sets his philosophical dialogue in a context which suggests the *Octavius* is to be understood as the ideal way to present the message to pagans. Clement of Alexandria tells us explicitly that the form of his *Miscellanies* is determined by his conviction that the gnostic view of easy access to the truth for the chosen few is unrealistic. He accordingly offers his message in reminiscences and notes which are like nuts: within the shell of philosophy one will find the meat of Christian truth, but one must work to get it. On the other hand, open discussions on the topic abound in our literature. They begin already in the New Testament period. The Apostle Paul writes with great concern about the dangers of speaking the word of truth through prophecy. In the somewhat plaintive protest of Clement of Alexandria on behalf of the "book," we overheard the see-saw of argument in Alexandra whether the message of the Living Word could properly be spoken in any medium other than the living voice. Lactantius, as we have seen, boldly castigates a century of Christian mistakes in presenting the message to the pagans.

In the second place, we should recall the creative tension between uniformity, rooted in the firm commitment to the traditional core of the message, and variety, springing from the personal idiosyncracies of the messengers. This is particularly apparent in the message to Jews and, even more, to pagans. The Christians clung tenaciously to the central themes enunciated by the Apostles as recorded in the New Testament. The message to pagans continued throughout our entire period to be a message, first, about God the Creator who was the one and only God and last, about God the Judge. In various ways, the figure of Christ might well emerge as the link between these two poles, though even this was not absolutely essential. In structure and content there is a striking similarity between the message of Paul to the people of Athens, and the message of Augustine to the people of Madaura 350 years later.

At the same time, the individual authors stamp their own

personality, prejudices and perspectives upon the message in the process of delivering it. Justin poses as a philosopher, Theophilus as a history buff; Tertullian takes the whole Roman world to court, Minucius prefers a dignified discussion among friends in an arcadian setting. Tatian makes no effort to conceal his anger at the insults he has suffered from his intellectual pagan colleagues, while Clement of Alexandria never wearies in his sweet patience. Perhaps more important, individual predilections help to flesh out and interpret the central kerygmatic themes. Compare, for example, Clement and Tertullian, contemporaries, one from the Greek East, one from the Latin West. Both express in some detail the meaning of the Christian concept of salvation. The western Tertullian appeals to the power of the Gospel for social rehabilitation. His message points insistently to the contrasts between Christian and pagan society, contrasts which imply that the Roman world must adopt a Christian social model if it is to seek truly its own welfare. The eastern Clement stresses the cosmic and personal aspects of the message of salvation. The Gospel offers above all an ontological restoration: of the universe to its original harmony; of the individual to his original relationship to God wherein he may progress to "divinization," to participation in the nature of God, his true destiny.

An important principle underlies this tension between uniformity and variety. While the Christian message invariably points to the one God, it speaks in very human terms, that is, in terms conditioned by our humanity, conditioned by culture, by heredity and environment. This principle, we recognize, is fundamental to the meaning of the Incarnation.

Finally, perhaps no aspect of our study deserves more reflection than the many ways in which the concern for a Christian identity entered into the message and its presentation. We can see the significance of Christian identity in the daily lives of the people we met in chapter 1. Our records witness to the sense of estrangement and alienation from their fellows which accompanied the Christian "sect." Like estrangements in general, this evoked both hostility and an air of mystery. Christians were viewed as a *tertium quid*—a strange species—and in the first three centuries the mere name of Christian became a sufficient charge to incur the ultimate penalty. In Tertullian's dramatic image the martyr's blood was "seed." We may assume the word was sown not only in that final declaration of Christian identity, but in all the steps that led to it: the different moral standards, the different social customs, the different political attitudes.

The sense of Christian identity was deliberately fostered among those who would bear the name of Christ, by catechists, priests and bishops. The message to converts pointed emphatically to a new style of living demanded of a Christian. It was, perhaps, too easy to define the Christian style of living negatively in terms of occupations or worldly pleasures—Christian teachers repeatedly forbade circus, amphitheatre, stadium and theatre. In theory, the message demanded a new orientation of the mind, a commitment to a new set of values, and it appears that many Christians failed to understand their identity in these terms. There was, of course, a highly positive note in the message of Christian teachers to their own people: the bearers of the name of Christ were also bearers of the Spirit of God. A Christian style of life was to accord with the ontological change the neophyte had experienced. Yet the very emphasis on the physical mystery might well deflect the average Christian from observing the demand for an intellectual reorientation inherent in the message.

It is, a little surprisingly, in the message to pagans that we can see most readily the way in which Christians struggled to define Christian identity in terms of an intellectual reorientation. In the second century, this call for a radical mental adjustment became in its strictest form a denunciation of the high culture of classical antiquity. The declamations against pagan art, literature and philosophy arose primarily from the fact that the literary and plastic arts had become the instruments of false representation, while the falsehood was not only one of fact but of perspective as well.

If pagans did not know the true God, their view, not merely of individual facts, but of the world as a whole was necessarily wrong. A Christian mentality had to be rooted therefore in an entirely different cultural ground—the world of the Bible. The Bible not only offered a true revelation of God, but a world of thought capable of nourishing the mind, and forming intellectual patterns intrinsic to a Christian identity.

Generally, however, the early Christian message modified the claims of such a stark position. Art was, after all, the product of intention, design, reflection, in short, of reason. The doctrine of one God creator of the world and of man, His image, forced Christians to acknowledge that reason was a universal gift from God, and that there could be no radical discontinuity between the Word of God, the divine Reason, and the reason of His creatures. On this view it was difficult to condemn outright the rational methods of Greek discourse, and the Fathers willingly followed the Apostle Paul in doffing the hat to the intimations of the truth the Greeks had hit upon.

No one, in presenting the message, carried this modified approach further than Lactantius in the *Divine Institutes*. He recognizes as valid in the search for truth the rational methods of inquiry discovered by Greek learning and he applies these methods to his own argument on behalf of Christianity. Moreover, he finds in the cadres of classical philosophy a legitimate form in which to present his message: it is Greek questions he is answering. The pagans have indeed gone astray and all their dogmas are ineffectual to change lives, but their mode of thought is unobjectionable. Herein lay the danger of finding merely different answers to identical questions, while the questions arose from a value system that remained unchallenged. It is perhaps significant that in his work *On the Death of the Persecutors* Lactantius identifies the persecutors of the Christians, above all Galerius, with barbarians. The time was at hand when a good Roman was a Christian and a good Christian very Roman: one would look in vain for a distinctive Christian identity.

Many Christians in our period were much more cautious. Some, for example, recognized that to whatever extent the message might be translated into the familiar categories of classical thought, there came a point when the divine illumination, transcending the normal modes of understanding, broke in upon the soul. The words of Scripture carried the divine power to secure conviction beyond our understanding. But it was above all Augustine in his *City of God* who endeavored to deliver a message at the heart of which was the question of Christian identity, and which understood Christian identity in terms of thought patterns and value systems. Augustine's great work is, in the first place, a challenge to the whole tradition of Greco-Roman historiography. He calls upon us to view history in entirely different categories. In the *City of God* our interest focuses, it is true, on the great centers of political power, but they acquire significance not through the majesty of their might, but as manifestations of a will to rebel against God, a rebellion cosmic in scope and transcending those temporal and earthly events which are the normal "stuff" of history. His message also calls us to a value system deeply grounded in a Biblical world-view. Augustine denies the commonly held assumption that power is glorious, and reveals how the pride of domination justifies itself by shouldering the responsibility to distribute a justice which is never in fact justice. The primary virtue is the humility by which we orient our lives about the will of God; from this and this alone spring the social virtues the Greeks have so long extolled.

Augustine's perceptive mind saw clearly enough that it is the mind-set, the intellectual orientation which not only gives rise to our value systems and the institutions embodying them, but to the categories in which we perceive our world. In his view a truly Christian identity is formed by a mind shaped by the Bible and oriented about God. In his message we can read the signposts on the road to a truly radical conversion.

DATE DUE

FE 13 '86			